The Lives Behind the Lines...

Other For Better or For Worse® Collections

Retrospectives

The Lives Behind the Lines...

20 Years of *For Better or For Worse* ®

By Lynn Johnston

**Andrews McMeel
Publishing**

Kansas City

www.FBorFW.com

99 00 01 02 00 RDR 10 9 8 7 6 5 4 3 2 1

ISBN: 0-7407-0199-1 (ppb)
0-7407-0209-2 (hd)

Library of Congress Catalog Card Number: 99-72692

www.andrewsmcmeel.com

Book design by Holly Camerlinck

The entire text for this book was written by hand
and is dedicated to Rod and Aaron and Katie Johnston,
(and with grateful thanks to Nancy Vincent
for deciphering my notes!).

Thanks, too, to the folks at United Media and
at Andrews and McMeel for pulling it all together.

Lynn Johnston

When I started *For Better or For Worse* twenty years ago, it was with a certain amount of youthful blasé. We had two kids, they drove me crazy, we had moved to an isolated town, and this was the perfect job for a show-off, a cartoonist, a would-be writer, a dreamer, forced to live in the real world long enough to change diapers, relate to adults, keep a home in order, and grow up.

The children were raised in the warmth and security of my husband's family. Rod's mom and dad lived a five-minute walk away from our home and were the center of our private little carousel. They and Rod were the machinery that made our world revolve with order and consistency. Rod's family was largely if not totally responsible for my ever being able to produce and maintain a daily world of fantasy, which I slip in and out of through invisible and undetectable trapdoors. In short, I am and always have been in a world of my own.

I do share my world. I'm a good mother and consider myself to be a good wife and partner and friend to a man who is so in tune with my moods that he can tune me in or out and loves me unconditionally. That security, that sense of belonging, that sense of being anchored to the real world is such a necessary part of producing a world that is imaginary.

To begin with, I thought I could do cartoons, make up funny characters that did funny things. Once you have signed a contract with a syndicate, however, there is no time to experiment. You have to draw and write and produce whatever is there in your mind. You have to do what you know and what you feel, and instead of looking for or making up characters . . . they come to you. They enter your life—at your invitation. They move into your home and into your head. They talk and can be heard in conversation—with you, with each other. They feel, and their feelings can be felt by you, or kept from you. They are sometimes frighteningly independent of the very mind that is believed to have created them. They allow you to be a part of their world inasmuch as you have asked them to be a part of yours.

My characters, for lack of a better description, came from my pens in 1979 as if they were caricatures of us, the Johnston family: a mom, a dad, two kids, and a neighborhood. The first names were all changed and the name "Patterson" happened because . . . well, I had a few days left in my development time to decide what to call this family. "Patter" means to talk; Patterson seemed to be as waspish as "Johnston." Elly and John and Michael and Elizabeth Patterson opened four windows a day into their private lives, more windows on weekends (in color!). And for twenty years, this family has grown, developed, changed, and matured under the scrutiny of millions of people.

I never thought about that at first. I still can't imagine millions of people reading and analyzing and commenting on the small personal revelations that the Patterson family shares day by day. If I thought about it seriously, my seat on the family carousel would fly off into the land of Valium and rubber rooms. I prefer to think that the Pattersons and I converse with each other and with my family

and with my friends. In fact, I always feel, when I write, that I'm talking to a friend.

The Pattersons seemed to be an insular bunch during the first few years. We were getting used to each other, and the goings-on at home fueled the fictional family's life with ease. It was easy to write a week's worth of strips in a morning. Kate with her sitter across the street, Aaron at school, and Rod at the clinic left me surrounded by the evidence of entrapment!

Toys and clothes and food and stuff. I'm a tight-ass clean freak, and living in a normal family atmosphere among all the normal family chaos gave me anxiety attacks. I'm not talking about the kind of thing that leaves you propped up on a couch wheezing into a paper bag thinking about the afterlife (which I've done), I'm talking about MANIC CLEANING binges that would propel me from one room to another, scraping, folding, dusting, arranging, and organizing stuff that would take exactly thirty seconds to undo as soon as the kids got home. Why? Why did I care if a cheezie sat on the counter for a day? Why did I care if a six-year-old's room looked like those police photos taken after a serious break-in? And why couldn't I be like people who let their kids eat a box of Froot Loops for dinner instead of a "well-balanced" meal? Who cares? Nobody's going to die if a vegetable is not consumed for twenty-four hours. Nobody's going to call me negligent if the Canadian (or pick your country's) national food guide is not followed to the letter for every meal of the week. People live their whole lives on rice and fish for heaven's sake, and I agonized over pieces of leftover stringbeans that I, of course, ate in order to save the world.

I was trying to save the world. I was trying to be the perfect mother: clean, organized house, well-orchestrated dietary intake—not to mention the OTHER guilt-producing, stress-inducing, self-reducing parental potpourri of school and quality time and fair dis-

cipline and . . . *fair discipline*?!!! Since when is discipline fair?!!
Rules is rules is rules. You pick a bunch that makes sense and you
stick to them. What's so hard about that? Still the plaintive, wailing
accusation, "You're *no* fair," kept the would-be perfect parent con-
stantly in a state of GET ME OUT OF HERE NOW! I WANT TO BE WITH
GROWN-UPS. I WANT A MEAL THAT DOESN'T INCLUDE SOMEONE ELSE'S
LEFTOVERS. I WANT TO SIT IN THE BATHROOM LONG ENOUGH TO
ALLOW ONE COMPLETE NATURAL FUNCTION TO TAKE PLACE UNINTER-
RUPTED. GIVE ME SOME FREEEEEEDOM!!!!!

This cry for help was what *For Better or For Worse* was made
of. It was acting out the feelings, writing down the complaints,
sending them off to the syndicate, and sharing them with other parents—who, to my relief and surprise, shared with me every morsel
of angst I was going through.

At home I wasn't alone in this picture. We're a family. We all
shared the zoo. Four strangers, brought together through circum-
stance, sex, and serendipity, trying to survive under one roof for an
extended period of time. We could have been any four people.
Birth, genetics, who looks like or acts like whom doesn't matter. A
family is a group of individuals who love, hate, trust, question, need,

console, and depend on one another as they grow and mature and learn how to give a little more, take a little less . . . all in the same environment, whatever or wherever it may be.

As I learned how to be a good parent, so did Rod. And as Rod and I learned how to parent, our two children grew. We accepted each other's differences (not always with grace), but as the days passed, the observations about being parents continued to flow into what we now called "the strip."

The strip wasn't just a coffee klatch between adults. It was becoming a story; a saga. And it was allowing me to be a child again. When I wrote from the points of view of Michael and

Elizabeth I was two and five and nine and twelve—whatever ages the characters were. When I wrote as Elizabeth, it was with her spirit and her innocence and her patterns of speech. As the children I could see, for example, being told to do something by an adult who was absolutely wrong. I could feel the terror of going to bed, thinking there were goblins in the closet and witches behind the door, because there *were*! I was Michael and I was Elizabeth, and in becoming these characters I grew up with them.

It would have been easier, they told me, to leave everything as it was. Keep the kids little; if it's working, why change? Why have anyone grow up? Well, that was never an option. Editors have as limited control over cartoonists as cartoonists have over their characters. The characters came from me, but I've never owned them. They changed when they were ready to change. Haircuts and facial features altered when the time was right—I was never really in control of that time. I would have loved to have kept the children little, but as our own two grew, Michael and Elizabeth followed—three years behind but always in step—year by year. Likewise, Elly and John Patterson began to sport the physical and mental characteristics of midlife baby boomers . . . stuck between stereoscopes and silicone, wondering what happened to just about everything they thought was cool, realizing that they too are going to grow old.

During the early years when Michael and Elizabeth were small, the strip rarely advanced past the inner goings-on of the Patterson household. There was enough material to keep me muttering to myself, scribbling bedside notes. But as the youngest players on the set became more sophisticated, other characters entered the picture—because that's what happens in real life. We make friends. We *need* friends, and some of the very best times in life are when our friends need us.

I haven't mentioned them yet, but from the beginning, the

neighbors on both sides of the Patterson family played pivotal roles.

You see, this really is a neighborhood. It's middle class and somewhere in southern Ontario, Canada. There are highways and bridges and schools and bus stops and a couple of malls. The Pattersons live on Sharon Park Drive. It's a crescent overlooking a ravine that follows the Sharon River. (It's a creek, actually, but in the springtime when the snow melts, it can rise dangerously.) This ravine is where Elly and her friend Connie walk their dogs, this is where the kids toboggan in the winter, this is the creek that April fell into, one day four years ago—but that's another part of this story.

Across from and to the left of the Pattersons' house is Sharon Park. It's about the size of a softball field. There's a children's playground and a couple of benches near the corner where the school

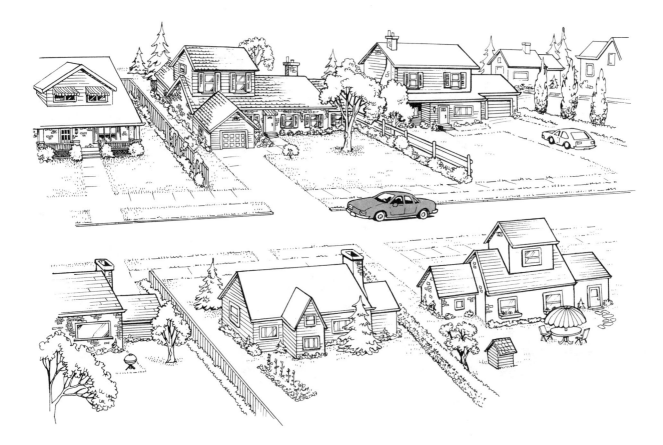

bus stops. From here, it's about a half-an-hour drive into town. Perhaps I should have a contest some day and ask for suggestions about what to name it, this "somewhere."

In my mind, this town is a composite of all the places that I have lived. It's a little bit like North Vancouver; Hamilton, Ontario; Lynn Lake, Manitoba; and now it's North Bay. Like Brigadoon, it appears out of the mists. It rains when I want it to rain; the sun comes out when I want it to. I have more control over this imaginary town than I have over the people who live there. Strange, isn't it?

John and Elly Patterson live in the same house they bought a few years after Michael was born. They've added on to it a couple of times, but it's the house they could finally afford after John's dental practice became a little profitable.

Elly Richards was a girl from Vancouver, British Columbia, who had always wanted to be a writer. Hers was the kind of family people would remember as being really nice people. "The Richardses? Well, they're terrific people, give you the shirts off their backs!" Elly and her brother Phil always imagined a life with a little less symmetry, a little more excitement. Phil wanted to be a musician and the two used their creative resources more often to pulverize each other than to further their artistic careers.

After high school, Elly made the daring decision to move to Toronto—2,700 miles east, away from her parents and everything she knew, to attend university, hoping to emerge with a degree in English Literature. She wanted, along with her education, the challenge and the excitement of her independence.

An enthusiastic and reasonably capable student, she met John Patterson at the campus library. He was sleeping in the spot she often used to study. He was in his second year of dentistry, and when he awoke he noticed her sitting there, watching him, smiling. She needed a small fracture repair on her right central incisor and could use, perhaps, three crowns on her lower left mandible. He was immediately drawn to her.

John was the first boy that Elly Richards had really dated. A couple of high school crushes had taught her about pillow-soaked Saturday nights when a promised phone call never came, and there was some impassioned fondling in the back seat of a yellow '59 Plymouth, but this was different.

As their relationship grew, Elly's commitment to her university degree diminished. In those days, the early seventies, you didn't move in with your boyfriend. Cohabitation before marriage would have destroyed the families back home. "Shacking up" was out of the question. By the time a year had passed, they were engaged. Elly focused her attention on an apartment and on getting a job to help

John, whose financial needs as a dental student were beyond the means of his parents. He already had a loan to pay off, and Elly's resources were stressed to the max as well.

They were married in a small chapel in Winnipeg, halfway between Toronto and Vancouver, the town where John had grown up. This was acceptable to all four parents, and the small ceremony was attended by family and a few friends. Connie Poirier, Elly's chum from university, was the bridesmaid, and an old friend of John's was the best man.

It was a quiet, unspectacular wedding, but what made it exceptional was the level of commitment between the two people, who promised to live together and accept each other "for better or for worse, till death do us part." Their honeymoon was the drive in John's old Volkswagen back to Toronto.

They stopped only twice along the way, to rest, to think, and to allow the gravity of their recent contract to sink in.

Elly left university to work in a bookstore. She freelanced, typing theses for other students, writing newsletters for a large Toronto firm, and even submitted a script for a play to a theatrical agency. It was never returned, and the copy she kept was put in a binder and set aside with the books and articles she'd saved from university. Something to go back to when there was time.

John and Elly Patterson's apartment was in the basement of an old brownstone on Spadina Street. Because the house had been chopped apart several times, to allow for the maximum number of legal dwelling spaces, theirs was an oddly shaped apartment. Facing the entrance was the cement combination shower stall and bathroom they were certain had once been part of a cistern or root cellar. To the right was a narrow kitchen with a two-burner stove, but around the corner, to the left of the kitchen, there was light! A long open room with six sliding windows looked out over a neat vegetable garden. A garden in the middle of downtown Toronto! This

long narrow room was the bedroom and living room, the study, and the repository for every bit of seventies student paraphernalia necessary at the time. A bed, a pottery vase, a small dining table with three chairs, a woven wall hanging, bedsheet curtains, and a bricks-and-boards bookshelf were some of the things that were "theirs." Stuff that had been acquired before the marriage was "his" or "hers" and included a flower-painted beer-keg coffee table and a set of Waylon Jennings records. These were the things that would always define them as individuals . . . and would therefore be subjects of "discussion" at moving time.

John's and Elly's families attended John's graduation from dental school. Elly should have been one of the graduates too. Her parents tried to hide their disappointment, but Elly herself was comfortable with her work, her home, and the potential future she'd share with John, now about to emerge from his dark cap and gown

with the wet, unstable wings of "Dr." attached to his name.

John accepted a position as associate in a small clinic in a town outside the city of Toronto. Working with an older doctor in an established practice was a great place to begin. John and Elly moved from the brownstone on Spadina, abandoning the coffee table but not Waylon Jennings, and set up housekeeping in a two-bedroom apartment. It had a bathtub, an oven that worked, and a coin laundry in the basement. This was luxury. This was also dangerous.

This theory is my own, and therefore unproven, but I believe that a two-bedroom dwelling instantly creates the illusion of "nesting space." Even if the spare room is piled to the ceiling fan with junk, this extra cubicle represents expansion, which sets off a hormone explosion that completely overwhelms normal female chemistry. There is therefore a certain amount of risk that comes with having a two-bedroom dwelling space, and Elly was twenty-four.

It was at this point in their lives that the accident occurred. Well, it's always called an accident when prescribed and proven measures of prevention fail. Elly's pregnancy was announced with surprise, anxiety, and frustration . . . which only barely masked the joy she felt inside.

John's work was paying the bills, she managed to continue her freelance writing, and a local bookstore had hired her part-time. Life was good.

If they had not learned how to save as students, they learned now. Every cent was set aside so that someday they might be able to afford the down payment on a house.

As Elly's middle grew, so did John's belief that, no kidding, he really *was* going to be a father!

It's different when you're the one feeling the changes, the movements, the expanding waistbands; for the non-pregnant member of the team it's a sort of "I'll get serious about this when it happens" thing. Then it happened.

Michael Patterson was pushed into the world red-faced and howling in the spring of 1976. Elly and John were far from prepared. Their parents had sent money for the baby, but they'd paid off a car loan and bought everything they thought they'd need second hand, except a crib. This they wanted new. Baby Michael came home wrapped in a hand-crocheted blanket Elly's mom had made. Tiny and immobile, he fit perfectly into the bottom drawer of their bedroom bureau, next to the bed he'd been sired on. It was a sweet and romantic picture . . . but dumb.

This is really where the spare room comes in. The next part of my two-bedroom theory is that a child's ultimate survival may well depend on the 80-by-31-inch piece of wood that separates him from his parents. A door is never so much a portal to privacy, a sealer of cells, and a barrier from bedlam as it is when a baby's lungs are in full frenzy somewhere between 1 and 4 A.M. It took the proud new parents exactly two days to move baby and bureau drawer to a spot next to the typewriter in the spare room.

Within one week, the entire apartment was rearranged. The typewriter and "office space" moved into the dining room, a crib was purchased, and the spare room was officially cleared for occupancy. It was Michael's room. They were a family.

Here's where my imaginary couple and their new baby become fuzzy in my mind. This look into their past doesn't parallel our lives at all—other than that Rod and I *did* marry when he was a dental student in second year, I DID need dental work, and the apartment on Spadina Street I've described was his.

In trying to piece together the backgrounds of these people I've surmised that Elly and John's five-year wait before they decided to have baby number two was for two reasons: one—they really couldn't afford to move to a larger apartment, and two—they needed a lot of time to adjust.

Michael wasn't your sit-in-front-of-the-tube-and-play-with-his-teething-toys kind of kid. He was a get-me-out-of-this-little-body-and-let's-see-what's-happening sort of guy! He was simply more than Elly and John had bargained for—more work, more supervision,

more time, more worry. He was your high-octane rugrat. Surprise!

With the changing of diapers comes the changing of friends: You no longer hang with childless couples, you gravitate toward couples whose cupboards contain extra butt wipes, couples whose mental states now permit a complete conversation to take place at the same time toddlers are being chased, monitored, sniffed, changed, fed, coddled, and catered to. Your routines change. Bedtime coincides with whatever time the offspring chooses to shut down and shut up . . . and for a few precious hours you're free from your willing enslavement, only to stand and gaze upon the face of your baby, now cherubic in blissful slumber. The bliss, of course is yours—and, with luck, you may get some slumber as well. But don't count on it.

"Busy babies," as we love to call them, often require several years of complete parental attention before one can even *think* of adding another chick to the nest.

This is how it was for Elly and John. As the mother of a really active son, Elly put aside any career aspirations she had to focus on Michael. She continued her freelance work when she could, and John accepted the role of sole breadwinner (probably white or whole wheat; this was before all the options).

By the time Michael was four, John and Elly had saved $15,000. It was a huge amount of money at the time and enough for the down payment on a house.

Elly's friend Connie told them about a home across from her house on Sharon Park Drive that was about to be put up for sale. The Pattersons bought the split-level brick home from the owners for $65,000. Even with their down payment, it was an impossible sum, they had little to furnish it with, but now they had a home of their own.

The windows we called *For Better or For Worse* opened into

the linear world of the Pattersons when their second child, Elizabeth, was a baby and Michael was in primary school. Here is where exact times, dates, ages, and factoid particulars once again fly the coop.

As a panic and deadline-driven new comic strip creator, I cared more about the gags (if I was lucky) and the drawings (if I was sharp) than recording birth dates and other time-identifying landmarks. I had no idea that this kind of stuff would ever be important! Nor did I think there would come a time when explaining who the characters were, how they came together, and what had shaped their personalities would be of interest to anyone but me. (This is a leap of supposition faith here).

So here I am, after twenty years, researching the other world I inhabit and discovering more than I thought I knew about it!

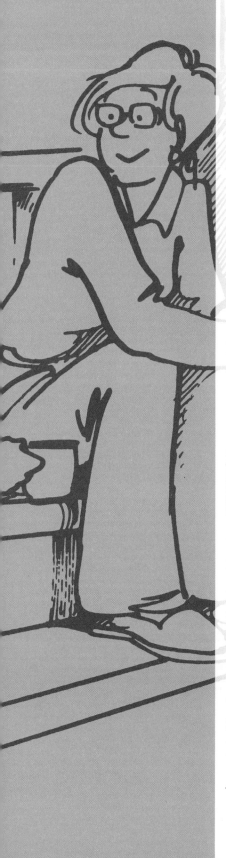

*T*he Pattersons' neighborhood friends first included Connie Poirier, Elly's old university chum, across the street, and Annie, next door. Connie was opinionated, abrasive, and designed to be sort of a feminist nemesis to Elly: someone who would flaunt her career and her lifestyle, someone who was, if not critical of, then slightly sorry for Elly, who had given up other goals in order to focus on her family.

This didn't happen. Connie Poirier wasn't strong and objective, she was insecure and in need of Elly's friendship. She was also a single mother, trying to raise her young son, Lawrence, without financial or emotional support from either his father or her family.

Connie and Elly had met in the long lineup for books and schedules on their first day at university. They shared a room in residence and a few classes in first year. When Elly left school at the end of her second year, Connie decided to go into the field of medicine and chose radiology. She graduated from college as a registered radiology technician. After a year at "Sick Kids" Hospital in Toronto, she heard about a group of doctors who were going to South America for six months, to set up clinics, teach local medical people new techniques, and offer free assistance to a large and needy population. She signed on.

The first of their mobile clinics was set up in Guaranda, Ecuador. Their unit of thirty workers—doctors, nurses, technicians, pharmacists, and student volunteers—was soon joined by doctors and nurses from the area who came to learn, to help, and to translate.

It was in Ecuador that Connie met Pablo DaSilva, a young medical doctor from Brazil. Pablo was charming and funny and spoke English well. He had studied in the United States, and his accent, demeanor, and genuine love for the people, his people, captivated her.

In the morning, long lineups would form in front of the school huts and temporary shelters set up by the volunteers. Patients who had walked for miles carrying sick babies in their arms, adults in hammocks slung between the shoulders of relatives, waited silently and in pain to be seen by the medical teams. A generator worked as long as fuel was available to supply electricity to the X-ray equipment that was under Connie's youthful supervision. She learned her craft under the stress of necessity, working closely with Dr. DaSilva to read the hazy images well. Often, they only had one chance to set the broken bones of a mountain child or to diagnose the extent of a head injury. They had to be right.

Their close working relationship quickly developed into a loving one. The light-haired, freckled French-Canadian girl and the dark-skinned, dark-eyed Brazilian became devoted to one another. Pablo was unlike anyone Connie had ever known before. His tight curly black hair, his cinnamon coloring, his laugh, and his language were all a part of the romantic image she had of this bright, intellectual, and hard-working young man.

It was not a good thing to do in the eyes of some of the other team members, when Connie and Pablo decided to share living quarters. In the remote villages of South America, however, where life is easily lost and everything seems to be for the moment, the couple didn't care. They continued to camp together as the medical team moved, six times in all. With each move they became nomads, leaving the world they knew they had to go back to, far behind.

Three weeks before the medical mission was to end, Connie Poirier discovered she was pregnant. Pablo promised that he would move to Canada with her and marry her. He wanted more than anything, he said, to be a father to his baby. He also wanted to make a pledge to her.

Papers were drawn up, arrangements were made, and Pablo kissed Connie goodbye at the airport, telling her that in just a few weeks he would join her in Toronto.

Secure in his sincerity, Connie came home to the city she knew and the life she'd started to forget and waited for her Brazilian doctor to arrive. He wrote for a while, but the letters stopped coming. She lost track of him as he continued to move from one outpost clinic to another. After a year, she gave up hope and realized she would be raising Pablo's baby on her own.

Connie's mother, a widow and financially well off, bought her only child a house on Sharon Park Drive. Connie's mother disapproved of everything that had happened and was glad that her daughter had decided not to return to Quebec. The house was called an early inheritance, but Connie returned to work at a nearby hospital and sent rent to her mother every month—to prove she didn't need charity, perhaps, but also to keep in touch with the only family she had. Within a year of moving into the new house, Connie married a man she had met at the hospital. Pete Landry was seven years her senior, divorced, and a traditionalist who wanted his wife to stay home. He was also extremely possessive of her and not at all attached to her young son, Lawrence. Knowing that the relationship between Pete and Lawrence was unlikely to improve, Connie worried constantly about the future. She also hated being confined to her home. The marriage soon disintegrated. A quick and unfriendly divorce left her single and in control again, but lonely and confused.

When the house across the street was put up for sale, she couldn't wait to call Elly Patterson, and when the friend she'd known for so long decided to move there, Connie Poirier felt whole.

When the Patterson family moved in across the street, Michael discovered Lawrence Poirer was just a few weeks younger than him. Unlike his boisterous and outspoken friend, Lawrence was quiet, analytical, and thought before he acted. He was the anchor that held a slightly out-of-control Michael down to earth, and the two

boys became like Tweedledum and Tweedledee. You rarely saw one without the other.

Although Elly Patterson knew about Pablo DaSilva, she asked Connie few questions. For a woman who was brazenly opinionated and wide open about just about everything, the subject of Lawrence's father wasn't something Connie could easily talk about. The subject of Peter Landry was also taboo.

Michael once asked Lawrence why his mother was so fair and he was so dark, and Lawrence said, "My mom says my dad was the coffee and she's the cream . . . so I'm coffee and cream—with lots of sugar!" This dialogue was never revealed in the strip and the subject has yet to be explored—but it will be.

Connie Poirier kept her last name. It wasn't a common thing to do, and it was one thing that gave her strength and confidence. Lawrence was the other.

*I*f you were facing their house, the Pattersons' neighbors were Anne and Steve Nichols on the right and Mrs. Thelma Baird on the left. Annie and Steve had a small son, Richard, and Christopher came later. The Nichols boys were closer in age to Elizabeth, and Elly saw a great deal of Annie during the early years.

Annie was a big-boned blond woman with a generous and positive nature. When Elly was asked to work at the dental clinic, Annie gladly took Elizabeth into her home and baby-sat. She was delighted to "have a little girl" and continued to be a second parent to Elizabeth whenever Elly needed some extra time. So Elly continued to accept whatever freelance writing work came her way.

We saw little of Anne's husband, Steve, and knew little about him except that he was a procrastinator and a collector of junk. Anything he thought he could possibly use or sell at some time, he put into his garage, leaving no room for the family car. Anne was constantly at odds with him about his never-ending plans for projects that were never even started. Scrap metal, used tile, car parts all went into his inventory, and when the Pattersons redid their kitchen, Steve gladly accepted the gift of their old Arborite countertop.

Steve and Anne were not happy together. Steve's job as a fabric salesman took him out of town often, and Anne was never quite comfortable with some of the excuses he presented when a later plane was caught or an extra weekend was needed in order to close a deal.

When their boys started school, they went to "separate school," unlike Elizabeth and Michael, who were in the English school system. Anne wanted her children to be brought up in the French Catholic culture of her family, and so the three friends saw less and less of each other, even though Elizabeth, Richard, and Christopher lived side by side. They had also started to fight. The stress between Annie and Steve was reflected in the behavior of the two boys, and Elizabeth soon sought the companionship of other children.

With her sons in school, Annie, thinking she was able to focus on herself a bit more, found herself pregnant with a third child. She and Elly became extremely close during the months that followed. When Anne delivered a beautiful baby girl, she was devastated to see that the child had been born with six fingers on each hand. She wondered why her daughter wasn't perfect. If her new daughter's hands were abnormal, what else could be wrong? Was it something she had done? Had she taken some dangerous medication or eaten something bad? She shared her feelings of guilt and fear with Elly Patterson who consoled her friend, telling her that the baby, Leah, was still perfect. And she was.

Immediately following Leah's birth in the paper, I received maybe sixty letters in all from people who had been born with extra fingers and toes—and other things too! Some of these letters were hysterically funny and some begged me to go further and have Annie's baby seriously handicapped, because this happens—it's common—and these babies live and are loved and they cope and survive and teach us that "perfection" is just a word that describes physical things. Some of the letters from people who had given

birth to special children described their lives in great detail and offered to help me understand and write about their challenges, their accomplishments, their joys, and their gratitude for having been given the gift of an exceptional youngster. I replied to all of these people. I wished I could have done what they encouraged me to do.

Leah had been born with six fingers, and it was an easily corrected anomaly. She came home to Annie's busy household and Anne soon realized that the house and three children were becoming her responsibility alone; Steve was having an affair. Anne confided in Elly, and suddenly, a dark wall came down for me. I couldn't see through it or around it. The fly on the wall was outside. No matter how hard I tried, I couldn't continue to document the relationship between the Pattersons and Anne and Steve.

Perhaps it's because it meant reliving my own days of "knowing but not wanting to know." My first marriage was like a board game that could have been called "Excuses, Excuses." For seven years I played along. It wasn't until after my divorce that friends and coworkers of my ex filled me in on the details of his other life. An unfaithful partner can craft some of the most artful excuses known to man. At some point in the drama, every excuse has been offered and analyzed. Even after all the evidence is in, and the ever-accepting spouse (now turned attorney) produces the ultimate evidence, there is still one last line that will stagger the most definite mindset. "Do you really want to believe that of me? Do you really think I'd do something like that? Well, if that's what you want to believe, there's nothing I can do about it. I'm sorry you see things that way." It's a brilliant strategy. I think there's some psychological description for when the guilty party deftly returns the volley of evidence and blame back to the accuser and the game goes on. That was what my life was like, and it wasn't until I had a child to protect

that I bailed out. If I hadn't had the guts to break away for my sake, I had the sense to break away for my son.

Annie and Steve's relationship was something I didn't want to go into; I didn't allow myself to go into. The two families drifted apart, even though they still live side by side and Elly still considers Anne a good friend. Anne, still coping with excuses, remains married to Steve. She is presently the catering manager at the majestic old Empire Hotel. Her job is both a career and a refuge. The boys are preparing for the last year of high school and college entrance, and Leah has, at the age of fourteen, taken a serious interest in the theatre. The house looks solid, but there are many cracks in the walls.

I don't know when the story will come back to Steve and Annie. Maybe I'm waiting for a time when I myself am less vengeful and more objective. It's strange to realize that after twenty-five years I'm still so disturbed about what happened to me.

*J*ohn Patterson eventually purchased the practice in which he had been associating. It's a small well-run clinic in a large medical-dental building, the kind with the smoke shop and pharmacy on the main floor and two elevators that take you up to various clinics, offices, and spaces for rent upstairs. There is also a cafeteria-style coffee shop at the back of the building in which many of the regulars have lunch.

John's most recognized staff member is Jean Baker. She has worked as his assistant and at the front desk. Other usually unnamed personnel are seen from time to time as assistants or hygienists, but John's private practice has never been a point of focus in the strip, except for the time Elly worked there.

Here we flip back into Johnston mode, because Elly's stint as John's dental assistant followed a brief time in which I worked as Rod's dental assistant.

I learned quickly, I thought. I had a good rapport with the patients, but I couldn't quite understand why the dentist was so impatient and rarely said "please." He wanted me to hand him the blue-topped thingy precisely when he needed it and he wanted the filling material shoved into this applicator gadget faster that I thought was necessary. In short, I thought I was doing a great job and Rod thought he should hire someone with whom he could be tense and abrupt (and not have to share the sack with them later).

This was a particularly personal series of cartoons, which garnered another stack of letters from other wives whose days as their husband's dental assistants had been numbered. We all agreed that the longevity of our marriages depended on our finding other things to do.

Dr. Ted McCaulay is a general medical practitioner whose clinic space is on the same floor as John's dental clinic. Ted and John have been having lunch together since they moved into the building, and, although they are not close friends, they enjoy each other's company.

An older and still somewhat attractive bachelor, Ted lives with his mother and talks a great deal about what he could have done or

should have done . . . if only. He always has advice for John, and sometimes John listens. Ted's appearances in the strip have been sporadic but very influential. He was once in love with Connie Poirier (whom he met while dog-sitting for the Pattersons), but it didn't work out. Elly surmised that this was because Connie was in love with Ted and was free to marry him. She wanted to marry him. It could have been because he was afraid of the commitment or of his acceptance of her little boy, or the voice of his mother telling him that Connie wasn't good enough. But he backed away from her, and she was devastated. For Ted, it's always been so much easier to want something you can't have.

When Connie accepted a job in Thunder Bay, Ted couldn't believe she would leave southern Ontario. This, of course, rekindled his interest, but she had made up her mind. After one abandonment, one failed marriage, and two disastrous relationships (the other was with Elly Patterson's brother), Connie needed to break away from everything and everyone. She put the house on Sharon Park Drive up for sale.

Michael, now in grade five, couldn't believe his best friend, Lawrence, would be moving away. The two were like brothers. They sat on Michael's front porch, watched the moving truck, and cried.

Although Connie and Lawrence moved away from the neighborhood, Connie and Elly continued to keep in touch. Connie's empty house across the street was like a mausoleum. So many memories, so many attachments. The Pattersons couldn't quite imagine another family moving into it, but Connie's house was sold to a family of Japanese descent. Carol and Keith Enjo and their two children, Brian and Dawn, helped to unload their furniture from the big van outside. The Pattersons watched with interest—especially Michael and Elizabeth who immediately recognized Brian and Dawn as being the same ages they were.

Carol Enjo is a nurse. She's an attractive, youthful, and gracious woman who enjoys displaying and talking about the many heirlooms she's managed to salvage and collect from her parents and her relatives. Encouraged by their parents to assimilate and not to learn their language or research their cultural heritage, neither she nor Keith speaks Japanese. It's something she's always regretted.

Carol and Elly, through the friendship of their children, quickly became friends themselves. Carol's Japanese dolls fascinated Elly. They had belonged first to Carol's grandmother and then to her mother. A traditional gift, these ornate dolls are collected to form an entire emperor's court. Carol displays them in a glass cabinet in her dining room. Keith, less interested in traditions and folklore, is an air traffic controller and a serious gardener. His flowers and vegetables are the envy of every green thumb on the block, and his annual efforts to grow the world's largest pumpkin are legendary. One year, Michael Patterson and his chums even planned to steal his best pumpkin but were thwarted by the fact that it weighed almost 200 pounds. I don't think I ever told this story. I should do it sometime.

So Connie and Lawrence were in Thunder Bay and the Enjo

family was now in their house on Sharon Park Drive. Elizabeth and Dawn Enjo became inseparable best friends. Michael and Brian became close, too, but not in the same way. Elizabeth and Dawn shared everything from their homework to their clothes to their most intimate secrets. In time, Elizabeth's need for Dawn's friendship became almost obsessive and she had to learn that people need to have other friends too, without jealousy, without a sense of possession.

Brian Enjo and Michael Patterson's relationship became more solidified when they were joined by Gordon Mayes. Gordon had been a year ahead of Michael and Lawrence in elementary school,

but failing a grade put him into the same class. Gordon Mayes was a survivor. The younger of two children, he was positive, quick-witted, but self-deprecating and always in need of a bath. His sister, nine years older, was more like a baby-sitter than a sibling. His mom and dad fought constantly about money and his father's inability to stay away from booze. Gordon's dad did construction when he could handle the work. He had his own truck and was a good carpenter when he was sober. The contractors who hired him knew when his good times were and gave him enough work to keep food on the table. Gordon's mother, Corina, worked for a dry cleaner. She was an excellent seamstress. One day, Gordon saw her put on a brown cloth coat with a fur collar. It was beautiful. She stood looking at herself in the hall mirror, lifting the fur collar up to her cheek as if she were modeling the coat for a fashion magazine. There was a cigarette burn just above the pocket on the right side and she knew how to fix it so that nobody would ever know. "If I owned a coat like this, I would take such good care of it that I'd *never* let a cigarette burn a hole in it—*never!*" she said. She didn't notice Gordon watching her. She didn't see the look on his face, nor could she know that he was thinking, "Someday I'll buy you a coat like that, Mom. Someday you won't be mending clothes for other people."

Gordon's father loved his truck. It was a red '55 Ford and it ran like the day he bought it. On the nights when he did not drive home from work, Gordon knew it would be another bad night. Generally, his sister, Ardith, would take off. She'd heard the arguments before, and she knew where to go to get away from them. Gordon was too young and perhaps too protective of his mother to run with Ardie. He would wait in his room, in his pajamas, by the door. He never knew if he would be needed to come between them. It was better that his father's fist hit him than his mother.

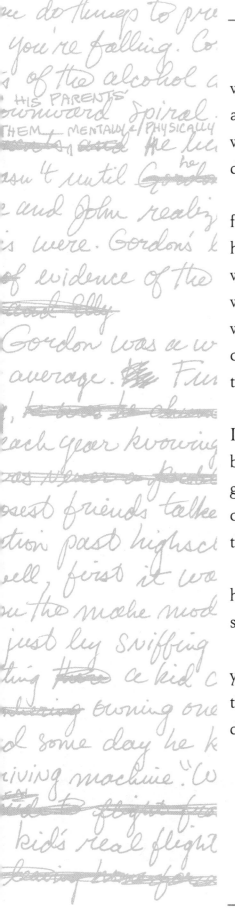

The strange thing is that, without the booze, Gordon's dad was a reasonable, even loving, father. He was a thoughtful husband, and his ability to tell a good tale endeared him to everyone he worked with. Few people knew what went on behind their closed doors.

Gordon's mother tried everything to keep her husband away from the bars, away from the liquor stores. If she found stuff in the house, she dumped it, but there was always a mickey hidden somewhere. The drinking, strangely enough, wasn't constant. It came in waves or binges. For four to six weeks sometimes, Mr. Mayes would be sober. His red truck would chug into the driveway right on time and they'd think, "Maybe this time, it's over. Maybe this time the good times will last."

Gordon's mother blamed herself when the binges happened. It was easy to do because his dad blamed her too. It was her fault because . . . Ardith had been born too soon, she didn't think he was good enough, he wasn't making enough money, and now, she was old-looking. Why should he come home to someone who cried all the time and was old-looking?

One night, when Gordon was in junior high school, he saw his mother take out one of the hidden liquor bottles and pour herself a drink.

You do things to protect yourself, to cushion yourself when you're falling. Corina Mayes found comfort in the dulling effects of the alcohol and slowly began to depend on it too. His parents' downward spiral separated Gordon from them mentally and physically. He became a fixture at the Pattersons' home, and it wasn't until he had a small accident with Elly's car that she and John realized how dissimilar the two families were. Gordon's broken glasses and bruised face were evidence of the discipline he was accustomed to.

Gordon was a worker, but even so his grades at school were below average. Funny and awkward, determined and strong, he managed to pass each year, knowing that he'd never be able to go to university. The fact that his closest friends talked about continuing their education past high school never bothered him. Gordon's passion was—well, first it was girls, and then it was cars. Gord could tell you the make, model, and serial number of anything on the road just by

sniffing the fumes. He knew everything a kid could know about engines without actually owning one. He had a gift. He was a natural-born mechanic, and someday he knew his life would revolve around the driving machine. Wheels. A car is the beautiful symbol of a kid's real flight from home, and in his mind Gordon had left home a long time ago.

*T*he first house built on Sharon Park Drive belonged to Thelma Baird. Its brick exterior, dormer windows, and generous porch are typical of the early fifties architecture. It was a family place, a warm and inviting house in which Mr.s. Baird, widowed and without children, lived alone. Mrs. Baird eagerly accepted her new neighbors when the Pattersons moved into the more modern house next door. She loved the noise and the activity of young children and encouraged Michael and Elizabeth to visit, often giving them snacks and candy just before mealtime.

Since the children's grandparents lived far away, she became a sort of surrogate grandmother and part of Elly and John's new extended family.

Mrs. Baird was from strong British stock. For years, she bred and raised sheepdogs for show. When her beautiful dog, Lily, gave birth to pups one spring, she hoped the family next door would adopt one of them. Then, from over the fence, she'd be able to watch one of her last babies grow up. Thelma knew this would be Lily's last litter.

Unable to resist the pull of a puppy's charm, Elly reluctantly agreed to accept a runt, as Mrs. Baird called him, and Farley the sheepdog, became part of the Pattersons' lives.

As a cartoonist, Farley the dog was an absolute joy for me to draw. As a writer, he was an easy addition to the strip because he never spoke a word. His emotions were readily displayed in his movements and expressions. Farley the cartoon dog was also, in my heart, a re-creation of my own dog, Farley, who was named for the outspoken and sometimes outrageous Canadian author, Farley Mowat.

Farley—the real Farley—was my first experience with the caring, feeding, and discipline of another living thing. Other than turtles and a couple of unfortunate budgie birds, I had never trained or been responsible for anything other than *me,* (which is an ongoing process, I've discovered).

So when my first husband and I adopted a puppy, I wanted to do it right. We went to puppy school, we fed him a proper puppy diet, we read how-to books about puppies. We were diligent and determined first-time "parents"—and Farley thrived in spite of us. Now, either we weren't quite clear on the concept of obedience training or Farley the dog was a dim bulb, because he never seemed to learn anything. He'd come if you tied him to the end of a rope and pulled, and he'd sit if you held his head up and pushed down on his rump, but he was lovable. He became a large, adorable, snuffling, licking, dust-producing, overactive responsibility. When our marriage broke up, Farley became mine alone, and I had a baby to look after. Farley was not fond of "the other kid" which was evident in the way he'd rev up in the hallway, before charging into the kitchen, where baby Aaron dangled like bait in his Jolly Jumper. Head down and at full speed he'd sideswipe the jumper, sending Aaron into a spinning, froth-raising frenzy, which I think he enjoyed.

URF!

KNOW WHAT, FARLEY?...

...DOGS ARE A GREAT INVENTION.

Lynn

I soon had to admit that this was not going to result in a friendship between the two. Either the kid or the dog had to go, and the choice wasn't easy!

I didn't cry when the young couple who responded to my ad in the *Spectator* came to take Farley away. I put his dish and his toys, his food and his blanket into the back of their station wagon. I gave him one last hug and didn't look back when they drove away. He had been a lot of work and worry, and it was a relief to see him go to a home in the country where he had more freedom and would be numero uno in the household. But his long hair was in my furniture and his photos were in my drawer, and it's strange how memories, like seeds, grow and blossom, filling your mind with colorful things. I missed him. I still do. I see his funny face and his bumbling body. I remember the way his mouth made a little o as he howled whenever I played my accordion, and I want him back again.

Bringing Farley the dog into the comic strip allowed me to do just that. I relived his puppy days and his growing up, and I discovered that cartoon dogs don't smell as bad, you don't have to clean up after them, and they are—if you work at it—fairly easy to train.

*M*eanwhile, back at the strip, life still centered around the Pattersons, so nobody knew when Mrs. Baird's precious Lily died. When she lost her dog, she knew it was time to make the move to a smaller place. A senior citizens' residence nearby provided the comfort and companionship she needed, and soon she was busy with Bingo and crafts and a boyfriend. Thelma and Ed were an item at their lodge until she died. She was the light of his life, he told Elly when she came to see him, and, at eighty-six, he planned to rekindle the flame as soon as his number was called.

Elly Patterson missed her friend Connie Poirier more than she could ever have imagined. Phone calls and visits weren't enough. In Thunder Bay, Connie had met and married Greg Thomas, an assistant bank manager and the divorced father of two teenage daughters, Molly and Gayle. Greg was quiet, gentle, loving, and kind. It took Connie some time to adjust to the fact that she was loved. Genuinely. When Greg was promoted to manager of a small bank in Connie's old neighborhood, she was numb with excitement. It was about this time that Mrs. Baird's house became available. Connie felt that the coincidence was too perfect. It was as if someone else had choreographed everything: her move, her marriage, and now her return home. Things like this do happen. They happen to me and to you we look up and say, "Who did that? " Or "This was supposed to happen! " Connie had always loved the old brick house with the big front porch. Greg and Connie bought and moved into Mrs. Baird's house and made it their home.

Michael and Lawrence reclaimed each other as best friends, which included both Brian Enjo and Gordon Mayes. The boys delighted in teasing Molly and Gayle, who ignored them mostly. They had troubles of their own.

Connie tried to be a good stepmother—hating the name, trying to love the girls. Molly was tough and insolent and sought the company of others who had things to work out. Her negative manner and her dark friends were upsetting. Greg, knowing Molly was pulling away, let her go, telling her that she could always come back, but she never did. Gayle, several years younger, tried hard to adjust to a new home, and new friends. She enjoyed Elly Patterson's company, and Connie was relieved to know that Gayle confided in

someone she could trust. Within a year, however, Gayle had returned to Thunder Bay and to her mother. It was a difficult time for both sides—the ex-wife, the new wife—and the girls in between. But people grow with experience, and painful times become positive. Molly is married now and living in the United States. Gayle is a student midwife who looks forward, someday, to having a baby of her own, and Connie is happy. She has their respect. Things work out.

Elly and Connie were reunited. It took weeks of intense conversation before the empty pages were filled in. They each had to know everything that had happened to the other (and to everyone else) since Connie's move to Thunder Bay. This is when gossip is glorious!

Here I've got to be honest and say that I love gossip. I lean into private conversations, I pry when it's possible, I'm part of the "neighborhood watch." With the confidence that comes with age, I can now walk into a convenience store and buy the *National Enquirer* without the compulsion to tell strangers I'm buying it for someone else.

Trouble with the *Enquirer* is that I'm getting too old to know who the players are. But I buy it anyway because I want to know.

In defense of this confession, I want to tell you that I also know when to keep my mouth shut. It's taken a long time for this lesson to sink into my skull, so I now have my RECORD button on at all times, but I'm very careful about when or if I'll press PLAY.

So gossip is a good thing, as long as it's about someone else, and Connie wanted to know—*had* to know—everything about Ted. Even though he'd made her life miserable, she'd never quite erased that charming smile, those cool blue eyes, his smooth flattery from her mind. Over and over she'd dissected their relation-ship from the easy way he'd won her to the easy way he'd let her go.

What was he thinking when she moved away? He had told her many times that she was the only woman he could ever love. If it was a lie, why was he so believable?

She didn't feel guilty about the smile on her face, that widened as Elly told her about Irene. As soon as it was clear to Ted that Connie was gone for good, he married his secretary. Irene had worked for Ted MacCaulay for two years and had, from the start, been guardedly open to his rather suggestive joking around. She was not unattractive; in fact, it's hard to describe her because, aside from her managerial skills and efficiency as a secretary/receptionist, she was surprisingly personality free. She did, however, have the strawberry blond hair, mellow voice, and slim athletic build that had so attracted Ted to Connie Poirier.

Their union lasted for six months. From what John could glean from their conversations at lunch, Ted and Irene's marriage certificate was a document of doom. Even before their disastrous honeymoon, it was clear that Ted's mother was not going to take second billing in her son's life, and her rejection, criticism, and interference hastened their inevitable divorce. In the end, the deciding factor was Ted's blatant indiscretion with another woman. Irene left their apartment, taking her clothes, her few pieces of furniture, and a stack of frozen TV dinners. She didn't leave a note. She didn't need to. Ted was heartbroken. It's always so hard to find a good receptionist.

Connie was surprised by the immense satisfaction she felt in knowing that her successor had not been a success. She was also surprised by the sudden ache she felt inside. After all that had happened, she still cared.

Connie Poirier was now happily married to Greg Thomas. He loved her and treated her with courtesy and respect. He was hardworking and reliable and he tried hard to be a good father to

Connie's young son, Lawrence. "What more can I ask for?" she said to herself. "What more could I want?"

Lawrence was in junior high school when he returned with his mother and stepfather to his old neighborhood. He was joyful in his reunion with familiar friends, familiar everything! Still, he had grown up, inside and out, and wasn't the child who had moved away to Thunder Bay two years before. He loved the action and the fun and the camaraderie he shared with Michael, Gordon, and Brian, but there were times he felt separated from them, out of step, somehow. Different. One time Gordon had weaseled a *Hustler* magazine away from a friend and the boys gathered furtively in Brian's garage to ogle the photographs. They made wonderfully lewd comments, laughing at each other's adolescent wit, taking turns with it as if, by merely touching the pages, this magazine bestowed upon them a first rite of passage. Lawrence took in the anatomy lesson with as much enthusiasm as the others did, he thought. But he found himself looking at the faces of those often innocently beautiful young women and wondering why they chose to degrade themselves this way.

The "in" jokes were about babes and bras and boobs. The sub-

ject of girls, and who had touched whom and where, filtered consistently through the hubbub of the gym class locker room. Lawrence found himself laughing perhaps a little louder than he needed to, and joining in the commentary just so he'd belong.

Puberty isn't an easy transition for anyone, and puberty was the other topic of choice inside and outside their school-ground society. As everyone was discovering what sexuality was, Lawrence was discovering what it wasn't. Nothing he learned in health science class or on the bus or on television made sense.

Lawrence was an above-average student, sociable and good-natured, and he had many friends, girls and boys. He was especially

fond of two of the girls at school and sought their company often. He loved their conversation and their openness and he treated them with great affection. He thought that surely he would feel that something inside that the other guys talked about, but it didn't happen. Not with them.

He had never been good at math. Questions involving physics or equations of any kind confused and angered him. He wondered why he needed to know stuff he would never use in his lifetime and why passing grades in mathematics were essential. Instead of concentrating on the lesson, he found himself concentrating on the teacher, how he walked and spoke and smiled. How he'd put his hands in his pockets and rock back on his heels when he was talking, and how he'd tilt his head just a little to the side when he emphasized a point. Lawrence was drawn by something he couldn't explain to study his teacher's every mannerism, and when Mr. Binder asked him if he'd like some extra help in math sometime, Lawrence felt his heart beat a little faster and said yes. Kenneth Binder was a dark, slightly built man in his late twenties with thick hair, an even white smile, and eyes the color of gray-green jade. He was attractive and expressive and an excellent teacher who cared about his work enough to know when a student just didn't understand.

Lawrence sat beside him at a table in the staff room. Mr. Binder explained clearly and carefully how the radius of this bisected the circumference of that and if you multiplied the square root . . . his shirtsleeve brushed Lawrence's hand as he spoke and Lawrence forgot everything. Mr. Binder's voice was kind and patient. He was wearing a pleasant aftershave that made Lawrence think of a cool, windy morning. Mr. Binder looked into Lawrence's eyes to see if his words were sinking in, and this is when Lawrence felt the feeling. It was like a sickness, almost. There was an ache somewhere around his heart. He felt it rise into his throat and he heard himself saying, "Yes, I understand" even though he didn't understand anything at all.

Lawrence lay awake that night, thinking. He had questions, now, that he couldn't ask. Any answers that came to him were awesome and awful, and he cried with the thought that he could be different from the guys he hung around with. Different from the guys in the gym. Different from the guys he saw last week at the movie theatre. They had joked about faggots and queers and dykes and gays.

> A queer by the name of Calhoun
>
> took a lesbian up to his room.
>
> They argued all night
>
> over who had the right
>
> to do what and with which and to whom.

Hysteria.

And now he was staring into the darkness, aware and scared and confused and strangely fascinated by the fact that he was attracted to another man.

For a while he dated Kelly, one of the two girls whose company he enjoyed. He convinced himself that he had been going through a phase. He'd been confused. "Everyone gets confused," he told himself. He'd walk with Kelly hand in hand. He loved her touch and her laugh and her gentle responsiveness to him. Still, he consciously watched for Ken Binder everywhere. Math class became his favorite. He began to excel in a subject he hated, and the words of encouragement he received played over and over again in his head. It wasn't praise, it was poetry. Kelly began to wonder why Lawrence's affection for her rarely went beyond a kiss, but Lawrence knew. He knew for sure. All of the feelings he should have had for Kelly, he felt for Kenneth Binder, and for two years

there was never any indication that Kenneth Binder was aware of this obsession.

For Lawrence, knowing for sure he was gay was like knowing for sure that he had an awful, and incurable disease, something so dreaded it could turn everyone you cared about against you. He grieved for the children he would never have, he ached for his mother, who thought she knew him intimately. He dreaded the loss of his friends, and he feared his stepfather.

So, what is love anyway? How could a feeling so instinctive, so unpredictable, and so overwhelmingly strong be so awful and so wonderful at the same time? Why was loving one human being right and another one wrong, and what exactly is the definition of the word "normal"?

Little by little Lawrence withdrew from the company of his old friends. He read a lot, and he learned to garden and discovered that he had a gift for growing things. He bought books about perennials and soil and how to garden indoors. He studied roses and, with the money he earned doing weekend jobs, he bought some rosebushes and they grew and he rejoiced in their beauty.

He began to accept himself for who he was and how he was and he resolved in his mind to be single and celibate for the rest of his life.

He was seventeen and in the twelfth grade when he met Ben Goodman. Lawrence had been skiing hard and fast and had gone, exhausted, into the chalet for a hot drink and to stand his frozen boots by the fire. With a cup of cocoa warming his hands, he sat by the window and watched the other skiers. There were the weekend families, the snowboarding cool guys, the hotdoggers, and those who had simply dressed to be seen. There were tiny beginners, and the mentals on rentals, and there was someone whose style and confidence stood out like a private jet in a used-car lot. The skier stopped, racked his skis, removed his hat and goggles, and came inside. He was blond, maybe twenty. The cold had made his cheeks red and his nose runny. He put his head back and sniffed, tossing his gloves and his headgear onto the thick plank table at which Lawrence was sitting. "Can I join you"? he asked, smiling. Lawrence indicated that the seat was vacant and watched Ben Goodman order a coffee and onion rings and a dog with the works. "You're a superb skier," Lawrence ventured, and the conversation began.

Ben didn't look like a pianist and composer, but he had been studying music since he was nine. He laughed easily and said how apprehensive his mother was when he did anything "dangerous," afraid he would hurt his hands. They exchanged information readily, surprised by how much they had in common. Ben's face and hands were animated when he spoke, his eyes widened with emphasis, and he didn't look at you but into you, sometimes. Ben was beautiful, Lawrence thought, and the feelings he'd suppressed for so long came rushing back. He felt the ache in his chest and the tightening in his throat and he tried not to let it show. But Ben's eyes continued to meet his and Lawrence didn't look away. There was a message and an understanding conveyed in the most subtle of their mannerisms and it was perhaps OK, he thought, to let the feelings he had inside just . . . happen. It was a Saturday. "Will I see you tomorrow? " Ben asked, as he stood and removed his tray from the table. It was a simple question, but the way it was asked made Lawrence's palms sweat. "Sure," he replied, the giddiness just starting to set in. And the relationship between them began.

Ben had had his affections returned by another man once before, but this was Lawrence's first experience. It took several weeks before they could trust and confide in and identify with each other enough to risk intimacy. One spring evening, they left the Surrey Street Theatre in silence. They were both fond of movies, and it had been an intense and thought-provoking film. They walked slowly, with their hands in their pockets, toward the lot where Ben had left his car. "I can't get the faces of those people out of my mind," Lawrence said, as Ben unlocked the door of his small sedan. The film had been about the Holocaust. They got into the car and closed the doors. Ben saw the pained expression on Lawrence's face and put his arm comfortingly around his shoulder. The touch became an embrace, and the embrace was freedom. For Lawrence, the awful image of what it meant to be gay was suddenly shattered. Within this spontaneous and tender touch was the knowledge that he could love and be loved and it could be true and

lasting and good and right. He wanted to cry but he laughed. He laughed and he cried and he laughed.

Michael Patterson was the first person Lawrence trusted with the truth. He had expected to wait until the time was right but finally blurted it out. His mother had just bought a puppy, to tide her over until the grandchildren came, and outside his house, walking toward the park, Lawrence told Michael he would never get married and have children. He would never fit into the picture his mother had painted. He was different. He was gay.

I've written more about Lawrence than I expected to, but it's a story that was never completely told in the strip. Those who have followed *For Better or For Worse* through and up to this part of the boys' lives will remember Michael's reaction, how Lawrence's mother refused to believe him, and how his stepdad threw him out of the house. It was Michael who knew where to find him. He convinced Lawrence to come home. Connie Poirier, realizing that her love for her son was more important than anything else, just wanted him home. Lawrence's stepfather, though unable to understand or fully accept what he knew to be true, agreed to judge him on the basis of his worth as a human being and not by his sexuality. *Que sera sera*. And so the new puppy they had not yet named became "Sera."

This part of the story is told in full in the collection titled "*There Goes My Baby*." It was written for my friend Michael Vade-Boncoeur, a comedy writer, performer, and childhood friend for whom my son and the character in the strip were named. It was written under the guidance of my husband's brother, Ralph Johnston, a talented composer, lyricist, and textile designer who, when he came out, gave me the honor of trusting me first. It was written for Douglas Brown, Dennis Weir, Rick Denney, Mary Stuart, and Bob McKinley, who will always be part of my heart. It was written because people are different. We're as different from each other as our fingerprints. In our lives, in our beliefs, and in the way we are drawn to one another for companionship, for love, for security—we are different. And some of these differences we may never understand.

Meanwhile, back in the make-believe world I find so believable, Lawrence Poirier has studied botany and he works at Lakeside Landscaping, where he excels in design. He is faithful to his partner, Ben, who is presently studying composition in Paris. He keeps in touch with the Pattersons, who are almost family, and even though he says he's different . . . he really hasn't changed at all.

*M*ichael Patterson was the kind of kid you could trust. Even though he spent much of his time tormenting his sister, escaping from chores, and raiding the refrigerator, the guys he hung out with thought he was cool. Oh, he could stand up for himself, and once in a while he'd lay into a good fight, but he was generally unfazed by the stuff that makes adolescent friendship an on-again off-again deal. He was open about his feelings, he said what was on his mind, and was usually good about listening to the other side of an issue. So when Gordon and Lawrence needed a friend, they knew they could count on Mike to be there for them. When the chips were down, even his sister Elizabeth knew he was on her side (unless, of course the chips were edible).

In the beginning, Michael and Elizabeth were patterned after our two children, Aaron and Kate. Although I kept serious personal stuff out of the paper, they can give credit to my job for helping us all to survive their siblingship.

When the kids in the strip were little, Michael Patterson had some advantages over his sister—but he didn't always recognize them. Being five years older, he could ride a bike and read and decide what he wanted for lunch, but his blossoming independence was often seen as a handicap. As an elementary school kid, Michael naturally wanted the focus of attention to be on him, and although he could be loving and endearing, his proclivity for pushing the envelope often pushed everyone too far. He was jealous of his little sister, and it showed. He was jealous of her compelling looks and her vulnerability, and he resented the way she was so easily picked up and carried and how she molded into his mother's arms.

Elizabeth sensed Michael's jealousy and, in typical kid fashion, responded by being even more endearing and even more adorable. (This trick is learned before speech!)

Subtle mutual resentment soon escalated into out-and-out war,

which Michael won with torment and Elizabeth won with tears. They had good times—great times, even—but a strong undercurrent of rivalry was always there. Michael began to see teasing as an art form. When the object of his affliction began to cleverly fend for herself, John and Elly Patterson found themselves holding a slippery rope in the never-ending family tug-of-war.

It's natural for offspring to fight. It's also natural for parents to want to drop-kick their darlings off an overpass, rent out their rooms, and take off to Tahiti (but anyplace with a beach bar will do). We've been there. The only time I ever saw my husband *really* angry was with the kids and it takes an awful lot to fire him up.

So, as our kids drove us precipitously close to committing illegal acts (in self-defense), Michael and Elizabeth wound and unwound Elly and John like clockwork. They were fighters—and not always on opposite sides. Brothers and sisters usually love each other with the same intensity that propels them to pummel each other into the turf, and young Michael and Elizabeth were true to the texts. It took quite a few years of maturing and the birth of a third kid in the family before they discovered that a real friendship existed between them.

In the meantime, Michael had a great life. He had a sense of security. He was a positive, quick-witted, and insightful kid who loved to laugh. He enjoyed school. He had a good family and good friends. He loved cars and motorbikes and video games that made you feel like you could fly! Michael loved everything that was fast. He loved skiing and cycling downhill. He loved the wind in his hair, he took chances with his hobbies, and he took chances with his heart. He was the first in his rat pack to fall in love, and despite their harassment he turned his attentions for a while from his friends to his fancies.

Deanna Sobinski was his first crush. As elementary school kids with elementary feelings, they prodded each other and teased each other, the words and the touching electrifying them, sending them into giddy bouts of laughter and silliness. When Deanna's family moved west to Burlington, Michael's mood was grim. Despite his young age, he'd discovered the magnetism that draws two people together. He wasn't too young to feel the loss when Deanna said goodbye. He wasn't too young to feel the helplessness and frustration. He *was* too young to know what to say or what to do, and so he didn't do or say anything. It would be fourteen years before he saw Deanna again.

Michael loved a good joke. Nothing lifted his spirits more than leaving a sock in the refrigerator or one last square of toilet paper on the roll, or dressing the dog in undershorts. He played an ongoing game of mutual humiliation with his sister, and when it came to summer camp the possibilities soared.

It was at summer camp he met dark-haired, freckle-faced, and moody Martha Macrae. Hormones had begun to swirl through the tissues of a much more mature Michael, and this encounter held the promise of more than just a touch. This was a possible *feel* if he was lucky . . . and he was.

Although his world still revolved around school, home and the guys, Martha had an impact on this strangely sentimental boy.

He wasn't the kind of kid who hung out in the workshop. He didn't know a crowbar from a wrench. When his dad offered to teach him how to build stuff, Michael preferred simply to watch. Gordon by now was headfirst into any engine he could find, running or not. Motors in boats, cars, and lawnmowers, even his own remote control car, Gordon disassembled with ease. (Assembly came later.) Michael just accepted the fact that things "went" and didn't care why.

When he was sent to his Uncle Danny's farm one summer, Michael became fully aware that he was a writer. It was to have been a summer of pleasures. He'd looked forward to hanging out at home, maybe making some bucks mowing lawns, but most of all he'd imagined what Martha looked like naked and wondered if this was going to be the year he'd see something for real . . . even if it was just through a wet bathing suit. Instead, he was sent to Manitoba.

Driving a tractor, hauling pigs, and learning how to ride horses was up there with pretty much anything a boy could want to do, but Mike missed Martha. Bev and Danny's farm was a few miles outside of Winnipeg, and Winnipeg was a long way from home. After the chores were done, when the kitchen clattered with dishes and the Manitoba evening sky held your gaze with its endlessness, Michael would get out his notebook and write to her.

He'd always kept a journal. He would never have called it a diary; what sissy-ass would keep a diary? But, a journal! Well, a journal told you when the last raise in his allowance happened and why, it recorded how his sister had once farted in church and blamed it on him, and other important facts for future reference (if needed). He put down important stuff like how beer tasted and the time he'd actually puffed on a cigar. It recorded his impressions of teachers, his frustrations with family, and his love for his dog, who

he often believed was the only one in the world who truly under-
stood him.

Michael wrote long, well-worded, and informative letters. He
told Martha about his work and his adventures and how much he
missed her. Sadly, she never wrote back.

When he came home from the farm he told her how hurt and
disappointed he was. Her excuse was that she was embarrassed to
let him read her letters because he wrote so well. It was a lame
excuse, perhaps, but also sort of flattering. Martha told Michael
that he'd be a writer, and he knew she was right. He just needed to
hear it from someone other than his mom.

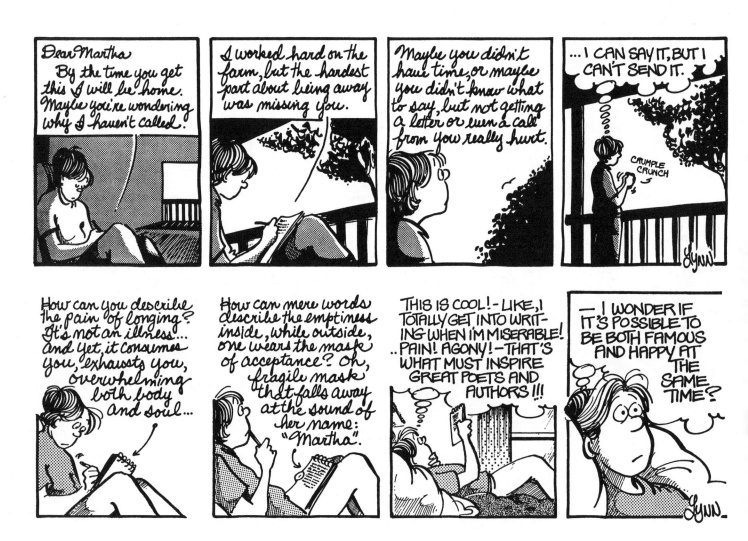

Michael's relationship with Martha became like a suction cup. You know it's temporary but you can't quite break its grip. The catalyst that led to their inevitable split was Martha's decision to dump Michael right before his driver's test. It was her fault that he failed. That's how he saw it, anyway. The glow was gone. Memories of all those feels he'd copped were buried along with the long, slow kisses. It was over. Could it be that what he'd thought was love wasn't really love at all? Michael picked up with his buddies again, got serious about school, started reading more, and got a good summer job. It was while stocking shelves at Megafood that he met Rhetta Blum, and for the third time in his life he felt himself being steered by some automatic pilot as his mind flew in amorous circles around and around and around. He wrote poems. His journal was now under lock and key. He felt "centered" with Rhetta. This wasn't just dating or going steady, this was senior high school stuff. It was the real thing.

For the first time in ages, Mike and his pal Gordon had something in common other than cars, action movies, and pizza. Weekends now involved actual dates. They developed an interest in breath mints and deodorant. They wore clean underwear and used aftershave and tried not to pass gas. Gordon, after years of having

crushes and being crushed had finally met a girl who liked him.
Tracey Wells loved Gordon Mayes. He didn't need to carve it into
the fence at the auto body shop or scratch it on a wall. It was there
in full and living color, and it was wonderful. Gordon and Tracey
and Mike and Rhetta doubled up to drive to the movies and the
burger joints and "around." Each couple would try and ignore the
other when they "parked" somewhere. One great place was a dead-
end road that led to a hydro transformer. It wasn't exactly lover's
lane, but who needs scenery when you've got steam?

    With another onset of *amour*, Michael wrote in his journal
that he now knew what love really was, and he did so with eloquence.

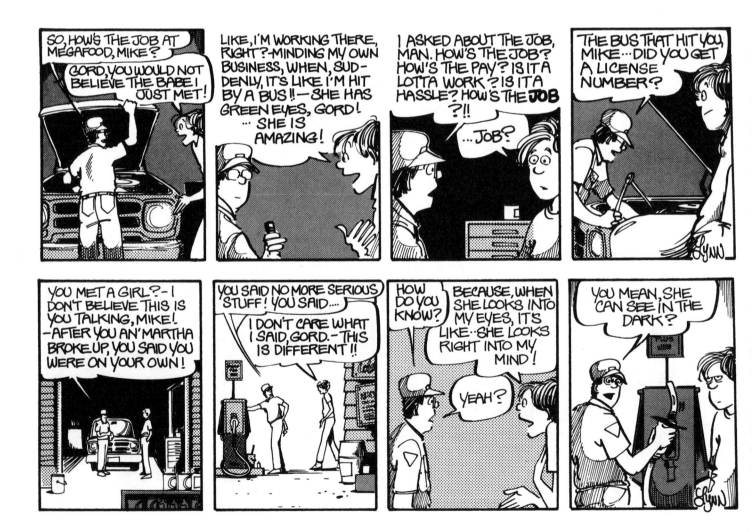

I've centered my description of Michael around the loves of his life because he's passionate and fanciful and capable of creating a world within a world. It was his relationships that first fueled his imagination. It was the rush and the awesomeness of being in love that compelled him to write. How do you describe a feeling so indescribable? Where does the feeling come from, your body or your soul? In learning how to write, he discovered that love and creativity spring from the same well, and to go there you must travel to a place somewhere deep inside yourself. Artists and actors, dancers, musicians, writers and philosophers and dreamers all know how to do this, and it's an instinct that takes time to control.

Michael was and is passionate about everything. His family and friends anchor him. He's discovered that he is much like his mother in talent, temperament, spirit, and drive. He was devastated by the death of his dog Farley, and it showed. There was a new puppy to chase and to run with, but Michael had grown up with Farley, and the pain of his loss was intensified by Michael's impending move from home. Leaving home to go to college was harder to do than he had ever imagined. Taking his teddy bear was a comical gesture, but it gave him comfort and peace at a time of excitement and fear and confusion. He'd never had the need to

leave home that his sister, Elizabeth, experienced. When he wanted to go somewhere, he could disappear into the solitude of his own imagination and stay for as long as he needed to be there.

Michael's life away from his family first began in the large dormitory building adjacent to the unnamed college in which he was enrolled. This college was somewhere in London, Ontario, Canada, and Michael registered as a student in broadcast journalism. The residence was worthy of its nickname, "the nut house," and Michael soon moved with his new friend, Josef Weeder, to a two bedroom apartment in a small private home. Josef, "Weed" to his chums, was a photography student with a talent for color and composition.

It was his ability to take unposed and deeply compelling portraits, however, that gave him an edge and a focus, and soon the writer and the photographer formed a creative partnership, each man's talent complementing the other.

Michael was now a man. Gone was the round face and the cool talk and the need to be "one of the guys." Michael was identifying more and more with himself, who he was and where he wanted to go. He decided that he wanted to switch from the college to the university (these are separate institutions in Canada) and was accepted, with the credits he had, into second-year journalism at the University of Western Ontario.

Now here's where naming a place or an institution in a comic strip can have interesting results. Already, I'd had calls from radio stations and the *London Free Press* when Michael was moving to the city of London. They wanted to know why and when and what in their city they could expect to see: buildings? parks? Could listeners or readers call in and ask for their favorite London landmarks to be emphasized? Could they run contests and have a London reader win an appearance in the strip? It was hard to know what to say, because the stories I write always center around the lives of the characters, and exactly where they were living was not something I had time to describe. Still, the folks I spoke to in London were pleased to have Michael Patterson in their midst, and he was asked to accept everything from dates to dinner invitations. I was flattered, and so was he. I chose London for three reasons. First, It has several superb institutions of learning. Second, it's too far from the Pattersons' home to slug laundry, and third, I wanted to have fun with readers who would assume that Michael was being sent to London, England, and rail at my arrogance. Happily, those letters arrived and my greatest joy was in knowing that the very next day these same nitwits would see London, Ontario, Canada clearly

pointed out to them on the map. It's the little things in life that are so pleasurable, isn't it?

There was some confusion when Michael switched from the college he was attending to the university. His roommate, Weed, remained at the college and has since graduated. Michael's course would now take four years to complete. I (Michael) received letters of welcome from the administrators of the University of Western Ontario. He's had e-mail from other journalism students and advice from some Profs. In fact, I felt so compelled to see him graduate from Western that I've had photos taken of Alumni Hall, the cloaks and caps, and the ceremony. This is where reality and fantasy

become a little intertwined. It's so much easier to just make stuff up!

Michael was in university, but in many ways he was still in "school." When Gordon and Tracey got married, it blew everyone away. Gord had managed, with the help of Michael's family, to purchase Daly's Garage, where he'd worked as a mechanic since high school, and that was hard enough for the guys to get their heads around. They just couldn't believe that good ol' Gordo had moved so quickly into the adult working world. He had a business to manage and now he was a married man! It had happened too quickly, and they weren't ready for it.

Michael knew this was a good thing. He knew these people well. He knew they were hard working and committed. He knew they loved each other dearly and would stay together. There was something so absolutely right about the decisions these two friends were making. Tracey and Gordon were the ones with the least education, but they were on their way to becoming the biggest success.

Michael was intrigued by his friend's new business. He wrote about Gordon and his article was published, and with the article in their hands they knew that they were both doing what they were meant to do. They also knew that their friendship would keep them connected, no matter where their paths took them, no matter how different their lives might be.

Michael was now a journalist. He was serious and sure. His studies kept him away from home sometimes for months at a time. His friend Rhetta, the girl he'd left behind, couldn't wait for him and became involved with a young man who worked for her father.

Once again, Michael Patterson felt the sting of separation. Once again, he wondered if love for him would always be like one of those afterimages that come when you blink your eyes: clear and bright for a little while, then fading into a jumble of color and disappearing into black. Memory holds an image like a photograph. He was tired of photographs and wanted the real thing.

When people saw that Michael and Rhetta were drifting apart, they were upset with me. "If you have Michael and Rhetta break up, I'll never read your dumb strip again!" One man wrote, "I guess we all need to experience a love that's true, even if it's just in a comic strip."

Michael's encounter with Deanna Sobinski was as much of a surprise to me as it was to everyone else. A young woman has an accident in her car, and Michael sees it happen.

In the hospital, later, he finds out that she's the little girl he'd had a crush on in elementary school, the one who'd left such emptiness when she moved away.

Like the serendipity in real life, Deanna's appearance was unplanned, but delightfully appropriate. She's a pharmacy student, in the same year of her studies as Michael, and both are preparing for graduation as I write. I want to tell you more about Deanna and Weed, but Michael's story needs adding to, and then there's Brian!

Michael is now twenty-three. He has worked hard with his partner and roommate, Josef Weeder. They have created a niche for for themselves in the competitive and changing world of photojournalism and, together, are about to begin their second story for *Portrait* magazine. Michael and Deanna have become part of each other's lives in every way. They're learning that love does have a definition, and that definition includes honesty, patience, humor, openness, flexibility, consistency, and respect. Deanna, although reluctant to commit to marriage, has told Michael Patterson that when she is ready to settle down it will be with him, and he knows she means it. He also knows they both have things to prove to themselves, and time and distance will pose no barrier. A loving commitment gives you wings and stamina.

Michael's family is more than proud of his accomplishments. For Elly Patterson, her son's ability to write and to obtain a degree in journalism has fulfilled the dream she once had for herself. Elly and John see their son on the threshold of a wonderful future, and he's grateful to them for his past.

Of the four boys, Brian Enjo believed he was the least artistic. Like his dad, he excelled in mathematics. He was a problem-solver and thought that engineering or computer sciences would form his future. By twelfth grade, however, he had started to research his family genealogy. He became close to his grandparents and asked them question after question about their parents and Japan. He learned about his great-grandfather's days as a cook for the British Columbia railroad, how the family had been evacuated to an internment camp up north, their possessions confiscated, their lives destroyed. He wanted to know why they spoke so little of the complex and musical language he should have inherited, and he bought books from the university library to help him learn. By grade thirteen, he had decided to complete his education in the old country. With the help of his family and friends in Japan he moved to Kawagoe City, Saitama, about an hour from the university he is presently attending in Tokyo.

Brian's sister, Dawn, keeps in touch with him regularly through the magic of e-mail. Her brother's descriptions of Japan, the people, and the history (which is visible everywhere) have made it her country, her people, and her history too.

For the Enjo family it has been both a loss and a gain. They wonder if Brian will remain in Japan or decide to come home. Still, they learn more each day about their heritage, and discovering one's family roots and stems and branches helps you grow.

The Enjo family came from two sources. When I was in grade six, our home economics teacher was a beautiful young Japanese woman, Miss Enjo. On treadle machines with clanking heads and bullet-shaped bobbins, she taught us how to sew. I still have the white apron she patiently helped me complete. She allowed us to have fun in her class, to enjoy the accomplishment of doing something well, and I will always remember her because she touched me. In her quiet, dignified manner there was peace and elegance, in her eyes there was joy, and her ability to connect with children was unparalleled. She made us want to learn. The name "Enjo" is for her.

The Enjo family is also the Masuda family. We have known Dick and Louise Masuda for many years, and the dolls in Carol Enjo's glass case belong to Louise! Stories of the internment camps in British Columbia are also theirs; they lost their homes and their property. With the pressure on their parents to assimilate, they lost their language and much of their culture, too.

Dick and Louise's house has the ambiance of both countries. Photographs of their sons and grandchildren cover the walls. On the tables in small ornate frames are the sepia faces of their parents taken after the internment. Delicate china, flowers arranged just so, and carefully matted prints of Japanese women in ceremonial costumes are some of the things I look at when I'm standing in Louise's kitchen. Louise can grow anything, and Dick, an engineer, now retired, loves computers and gadgets and really bad jokes.

Rod and I have had the pleasure of visiting Tokyo, but any insights I might have into the lives of the Enjo family come from Dick and Louise Masuda, and I thank them so much.

*E*lizabeth Patterson was made to order. If Elly and John had written down everything they'd wanted in a little girl, Elizabeth would have arrived, just so and gift-wrapped.

Round and pink with blue eyes and curling blond hair, she looked like pictures taken of her older brother, five years ago. She came home from the hospital in the arms of her mother, her daddy carrying the flowers and gifts that seemed to magically appear when she did.

Her brother, Michael, was excited but wary as he parted the soft pink blanket and stared at the newcomer. That is to say, he was eager to celebrate a momentous occasion but wondered if sharing his parents with someone else would work out.

Michael was five. In five years Elly and John had forgotten what a new baby does to both sleep and psyche and learned once again the art of parenting something that can't be reasoned with.

Unlike her brother, Elizabeth slept well. She ate things that Michael would have hidden in his pant cuffs, laughed readily, and appeared to be an easy kid to live with.

For some reason, Elizabeth was very shy outside the family. Even relatives were kept at bay. She needed time to watch and assess and accept everyone. She was therefore slow to make friends, preferring to stand and watch the neighborhood children and wait for the invitation before she'd join in. Once she felt safe and secure, she befriended people with unrestrained loyalty.

As she passed from the baby stage into the wobbly world of preschool, home was heaven except for the days when, out of jealousy or boredom, Michael teased her . . . and he was good at it.

Squabbling with her older brother soon taught her to fend for herself. She learned that kids play with each other's toys as creatively as they play with each other's feelings, and that life outside the Patterson family yard wasn't easy.

When Elly returned to work part time, Elizabeth was placed in the loving care of her mother's friend and neighbor, Anne Nichols. Annie and Steve's two boys, Christopher and Richard, were her first constant playmates. Like her brother, however, the boys resented her invasion of their turf. It was clear that their mother, too, was delighted to have a little girl in the family. Annie began to dote on Elizabeth.

Richard and Chris were boisterous and loud and eager to roughhouse, often teasing her a little too much, pushing her a little too hard. Elizabeth retaliated with words—and discovered that they could hurt more than sticks and stones. A moratorium was established and the three youngsters played together, tolerated one another, and even enjoyed each other's company. They had no choice.

With her entrance into kindergarten, the relationship "Lizzie" had with Annie's boys changed forever. Richard and Christopher had been enrolled in the separate Catholic school system and Elizabeth was sent to public school. They were still neighbors, they would still see a lot of each other, but attending different schools would separate them both mentally and physically.

Even though they'd never been the closest of friends, she missed the boys. She knew where she stood with them, knew how to handle—even manipulate—them, and now the shyness and withdrawal was coming back.

She sucked her thumb at night. She clung to her mother and cried as she was led into the bright schoolroom with its colorful pictures and tiny furniture, just her size. This beautiful and inviting

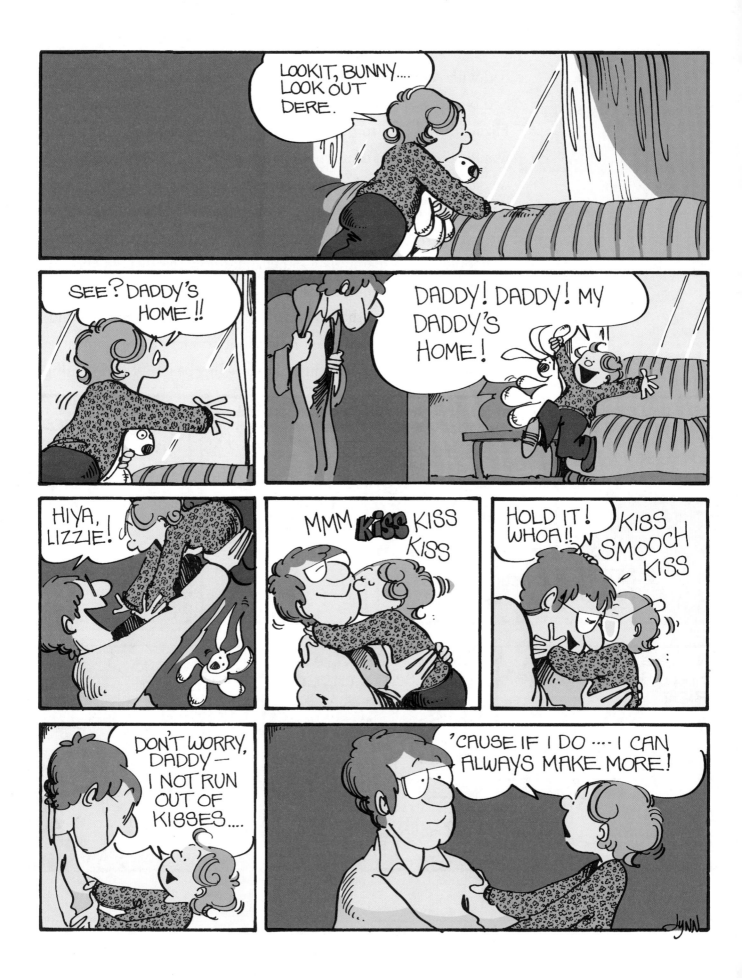

room was full of strangers.

In time, she let go. Little by little she allowed other kids into her world. She trusted the teachers and adjusted to the routine of leaving home and spending time outside the neighborhood. On the day she rode in the school bus alone for the very first time, she couldn't stop talking. She talked to everyone.

Elizabeth began to understand how her brother ticked and how to bug him effectively without detection. Being cute was a definite advantage. It was easy to convince Mom and Dad that she was the underdog, and they generally fell for it—especially Dad.

Elizabeth adored her dad. To her he was sunshine and laughter and everything wonderful. In the evening, she would wait for the sound of his car in the driveway. She'd time her running embrace with the exact moment the door was fully open, and he'd pick her up as if she weighed nothing at all and swing her high before hugging her tight to his chest. With her face buried in the collar of his overcoat, the scent of his skin, his hair, and the dental clinic filled her with the joyful satisfaction of knowing that Dad was really home.

As a small child, Lizzie was closer to her dad than just about anyone. Her mom was a little hurt when the toddler who'd clung to

her for security now jumped into the arms of her dad when he came home—and stayed there. It wasn't a big hurt, just a wistful sort of thing, and she pushed it aside, knowing that bonds like this are natural and good. She encouraged it.

On the other hand, Michael had been drawing closer to Elly. They shared the same reverence for books and good movies and poems by Shel Silverstein. Michael preferred making something in the kitchen to making something in the workshop, and a tiny, almost insignificant sting could be felt in John's heart if an offer to do something with Michael was turned down.

Subtle family feelings go round and round like a wheel, each spoke supporting a thought, a reason, an attitude, a fear. The spokes in the Pattersons' wheel included the feelings they had for each other and the awareness they had of themselves, and they tried hard to keep everything balanced by talking and loving and admitting when they were hurt or had hurt someone else. Nothing heals a wound faster than an apology.

Lizzie was comfortable with the kids at school but didn't have a really close friend until Dawn Enjo moved into Connie Poirier's old house across the street.

$\mathcal{D}$awn was slim with blue-black hair, expressive eyes, and a grin that captivated. She was the exact same age as Elizabeth. She talked the same, she laughed at the same things, and liked the same stuff. She had the same games and the same toys. She liked pineapple pizza and light-up sneakers, and they both confessed that if they ever met Jonathan Taylor Thomas in person, they'd actually and totally die!

In Dawn, Elizabeth found a soulmate, a girlfriend with whom she could share everything from sandals to secrets. They both suffered the crushing blow of being born second, to having brothers five years older who made their lives a drag!

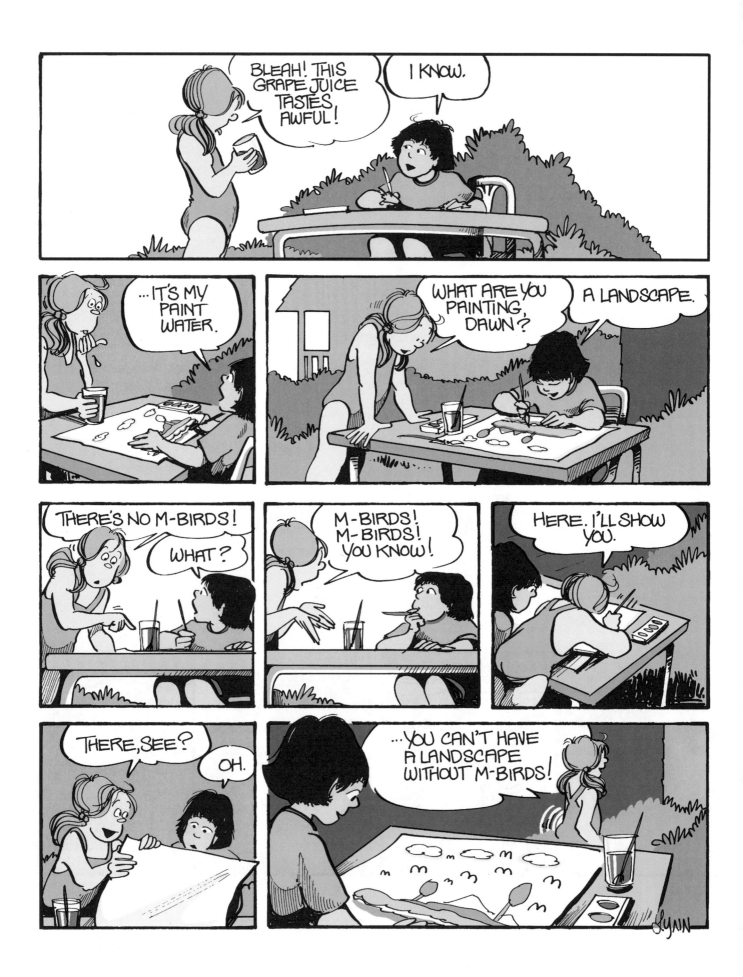

The Enjos and the Pattersons wondered how long this closeness would last; after all, there were other kids out there—but Lizzie and Dawn were rarely seen apart at school or on Sharon Park Drive. They were like "chosen" sisters.

Elizabeth was the first to sprout some evidence of womanhood, and the purchase of her first bra was a historic event. Elly bought her two, one to wash and one to wear. The extra immediately went to Dawn, who found several silk handkerchiefs to stuff into it.

With their bogus bosoms thrust forward, the two girls strutted up and down the street. It didn't matter that the bumps under their

T-shirts weren't exactly even in placement or size, they were women and they wanted to be noticed . . . and they were.

"Training bras?" their brothers shouted loud enough for neighbors to hear. "What are you training them to do?!" And Michael and Brian propped themselves on their road hockey sticks, convulsed with laughter.

That same day, Michael discovered his jockstrap had been fired onto the telephone wires that spanned the nearest intersection. It hung there, waving in the wind, testimony to tits over testosterone. Such victories are sweet.

Elizabeth could now retaliate. The names her brother called

her—Lizardbreath, Lizardbutt, Dizzy busy fizzy Lizzie, sistwirp—
went by unnoticed. She had long given up any efforts to rhyme
something—anything with the word Michael, but "ugly brother"
seemed to hit a nerve. Insult for insult, slug for slug, they were even.

The conversations Elizabeth and Dawn had with friends at
school now focused mainly on guys. They talked about looks and
fashions, makeup and weight. The two girls began to try out new
relationships and hung around with some of the tough kids, the
moody kids, the outcasts. They connected with a provocative and
volatile girl called Candace, who smoked and never ate anything
and was angry about everything. Candace was cool. She gave them
cigarettes and told them stuff about sex that they never could have
imagined. Candace talked openly about pills and puberty, and they
wondered how somebody so young could possibly know so much.

When a body morphs from kid-to-adult, stuff grows at weird
times and in weird places. Comparisons, furtive and otherwise, in
the girls change rooms revealed a wide range of "developments."
Candace encouraged Liz and Dawn to compare their progress:

who had the most armpit hair; any cramps yet? Did anyone have a bra who really *needed* one? Height, weight, shape, and size were scrutinized for signs of maturing femininity, and Elizabeth soon decided that she was trailing them all. Dawn was gravitating more toward Candace, and on top of this, Elizabeth needed glasses. She was having trouble with zits, and her dad had discovered she still sucked her thumb occasionally—enough to affect her teeth! It was a secret she'd hidden for years.

He installed an appliance in her mouth to curb the habit, and the addition of one more insult made Elizabeth withdraw again into the protective childhood shell she had kept just in case she needed it.

The appliance affected her speech. How could she explain what it was? It wasn't braces. She decided to just live with it and put up with the questions kids asked.

Elizabeth was now in junior high school. Hormones made her irritable. Her shyness and self-consciousness returned. She didn't fit into the image she saw of teens in the magazines, and she felt left out of the group that Dawn was now part of. Elizabeth couldn't quite put her feelings into words, she just knew in her heart she was ugly.

At home, she got along well with her family, but Elly knew something was bothering her. Liz gravitated more and more to the television and to the dog. She'd coax him onto her lap and hug him in silence. "What is it?" Elly would say, "Is it something you can tell me?" But Elizabeth would shrug and shake her head. It's hard to describe how you feel when you're not quite sure yourself.

Sharon Edwards, Elizabeth's math teacher, recognized in her student something familiar. She saw the pensiveness and the withdrawal, the bitterness in being teased and singled out. The appliance in Elizabeth's mouth made her different enough to become target practice, and Elizabeth had lost her will to fight back.

Sharon had lived with difference for a good part of her life. When she was sixteen, she accepted a ride on a motorcycle. It was going to be a fast tear around the block. Within minutes, though, she and the driver, a young man she hardly knew, were out of control, the wheels of the bike skidding on loose gravel. Teeth clenched, bodies taut, they braced themselves as the front wheel rolled up onto a wedge of concrete guardrail; the driver instinctively swerved left. Sharon fell to the right, the cuff of her pant leg caught on metal; it held her, suspended for a second, and then she landed hard, her spine cracking against the hump of cement that was, ironically, put there for safety.

Athletic, active, and outgoing, Sharon Edwards did not accept the fact that she would now be "handicapped." The first wheelchair was cumbersome and ugly. She resented the sympathy and the questions it solicited, and she hated those who treated her as if she weren't there.

Still, there was no future in self pity, and "handicapped" by no means meant incapable. She discovered her strength through athletics. She willed herself to succeed. She finished high school with honors and got her teaching degree, specializing in math and science. She bought a special van and a chair just for sports. She went kayaking and she raced and her body became part flesh and part steel. She even fell in love with a man who loved her and accepted her, challenges and all. Although they've never married, they have a partnership and an understanding that transcends any physical boundaries—and Miss Edwards, the teacher in the wheelchair, considers herself lucky in many ways.

Sharon Edwards recognized herself in Elizabeth Patterson and took the time to find out why. Her counsel was straightforward and her support was sincere. Elizabeth felt privileged to be with her and allowed all of the pent up fears and frustrations to come pouring

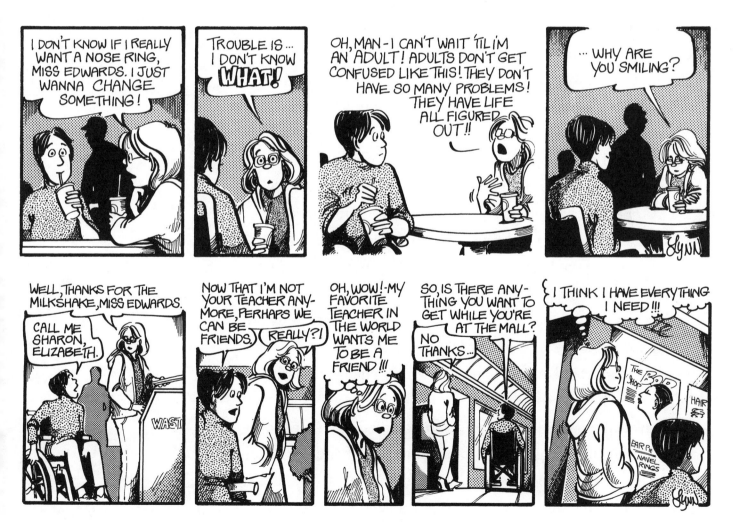

out. She sought out Miss Edwards's company after school, helping with paperwork, carrying books to her car, and felt she was learning more from her now than she had learned in all the science and math classes she had taken.

She quoted Miss Edwards often. At home, "Miss Edwards said" seemed to precede every sentence.

Her mother wondered in silence why she was not the one Elizabeth was turning to, but was glad that her daughter had someone to guide her and was grateful for the positive changes she saw.

When I was in grade eight I took my troubles to a young teacher who listened without lecturing, who gave me the courage to believe in myself at a time when I felt lost and confused about everything. Thérèse Thériault was our drama teacher. I would have done anything for her. She was once lectured by the principal for allowing us to call her by her first name during rehearsals after school, but she continued to let us see her as "human" and approachable. She gave us the freedom to speak out, say what we thought—and she respected our ideas, our feelings, and our abilities. We adored her. Because she gave so much to us, the students gave 100 percent back to her. She's probably forgotten me (and Michael VadeBoncoeur and Paul Willis and Ellie Grin . . .), but I've kept photographs of her, I still remember the poems she had us memorize, and when I see my reflection I sometimes think I see her. She was exceptional, and I often wonder how many of us owe grateful thanks to teachers like Thérèse Thériault. How wonderful it would be if we could let them know how they changed our lives and made us better people.

Elizabeth was definitely demonstrating the "addle" in adolescence. Elly felt a tearing separation between herself and her daughter and tried hard to spend more time with her, talking less and listening more. Candace and Dawn still chummed with Elizabeth.

Like shells on a beach, they drifted together, then drifted apart with the rise and fall of emotional tides.

A young man named Anthony Caine had become a constant in her life: kind of nerdy, kind of neat, but smart and reliable and he liked her a lot. When Elizabeth admitted to her mother that she sort of liked him too, Elly was delighted. A door had opened! Elizabeth was coming back.

The fact is, the Patterson house had always been an open-door kind of place. The kids felt comfortable bringing friends home, anytime. Elly and John enjoyed and encouraged the activity that went on in their rec room almost unsupervised. Elizabeth had joined the school choir (where she'd met Anthony, I suspect), and the girls were no longer influenced by Candace. Elizabeth skated and swam and sewed and her friends were easygoing, now, and fun to have around.

Things were beginning to settle down. With hormones in harmony, she could accompany her mother to a mall without embarrassment. In fact she had concluded that Mom was OK—even *majorly* OK. They could talk now, woman to woman, girl to girl. Elizabeth poured stuff out to Elly that she used to save for her buddies. Mother and daughter felt closer than they'd ever been before.

In the middle of this progress, Elly discovered she was pregnant. The announcement caught everyone off guard. "Two is company, three's a crowd," thought Elly—and Michael and Elizabeth had been less than harmonious company.

Both kids were definitely grossed out at the thought of their mother giving birth. Pregnancy was definite evidence that their parents still "did it" and neither of them could imagine the fogies fondling, much less making love!

April Marian's arrival was welcome and exciting, but it changed everything. Again. Elizabeth was now the kid in the middle, and although she felt protective and loving toward her new sister, it put her into the category of "sitter" as well.

Once more, the adult relationship she was beginning to enjoy with her mother was on hold. Elly went back to work when April was old enough for day care, and Elizabeth's responsibilities escalated.

With her older brother in college, she was part-time kid, part-time cook and caregiver. Elly and John tried to be fair and flexible, but they needed her. She had an important role to play. This made Elizabeth responsible, but resentful as well.

Elizabeth entered high school with confidence. The appliance was gone, the glasses now contacts; she was another bug who'd turned into a butterfly.

The first long trip she took alone was to Winnipeg. Visits to Aunt Bev and Uncle Danny were an educational experience the Patterson kids looked forward to. It meant horses and tractors, long dusty back roads, and if you climbed a tree you could see forever.

Elizabeth's cousin, Laura, was the same age, and this time they greeted each other with a strong, mature hug and adult conversation. They weren't kids anymore. Laura taught Elizabeth how to drive and how to ride. Out on the prairie she saw in her mind's eye

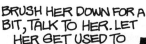

the vastness of Canada and wondered what she would add to this country. What would she be doing in ten years . . . twenty? "Teacher's college," she said to herself. It wasn't a question, it was an answer, and she realized that her friendship with Sharon Edwards had probably been the greatest turning point in her life.

The girls worked hard. Elizabeth felt at home in the small town, with its grain elevator, general store, machine shop, and bar. They went to dances and they went to a country auction, from which Laura and Elizabeth emerged with a large white rabbit.

Elizabeth went home to Ontario brown and freckled, carrying an animal cage. April was thrilled to have a rabbit in the house; Elly

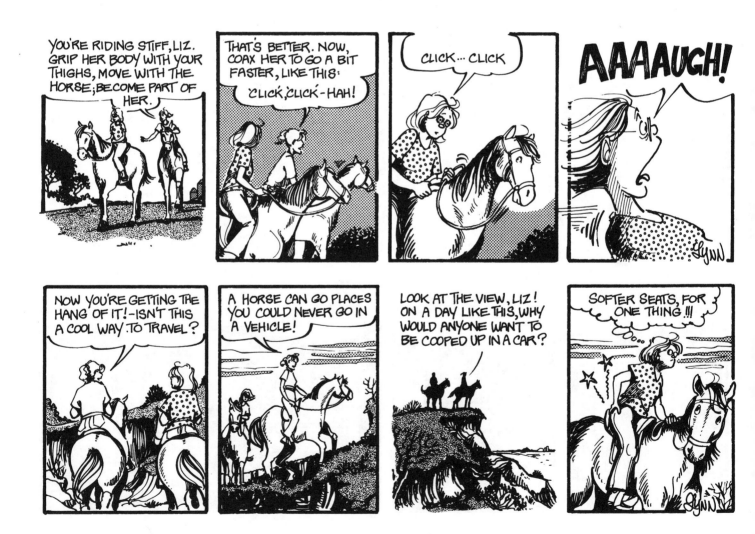

was not. Nonetheless, Sheldon F. Bunsworthby (F for Fuzzlewhite) joined the family dog, the goldfish, turtles, and whatever April brings in from outside as another member of the family zoo. The rabbit has always been referred to as Mr. B.; his full name is much too formal, I think.

Elizabeth graduated from high school the year her grandmother died. The family mourned Grandma Marian's passing and Elizabeth gave up her bedroom to her grandfather, who came to stay until his grief was manageable and he could decide what to do with himself, with his life, with his future.

As a gift to her grandmother, Elizabeth sang "Climb Every

Mountain" at her memorial service and John wondered how she could sing so well and so courageously, her voice unfaltering and her expression serene. But Elizabeth was listening to the message in Grandma Marian's favorite song, and as the words vibrated in her throat, she felt herself climbing every mountain, fording every stream, following every rainbow. She has a dream.

Elizabeth is now eighteen years old. She cares deeply for Anthony and still considers Dawn Enjo her closest friend. She's applying to university in preparation for a teaching degree and meets Sharon Edwards from time to time just to talk. She adores her little sister, even though April uses her stuff and drives her crazy, and, although she's ready to leave them, she loves her parents very much. The two people who mean the most to her, the two people who nurtured her, fought with her, loved her, and were there for her through triumph and trial are prepared to let her go.

The kid who once seemed like the easiest to raise had been the most difficult of all. Elizabeth knows it's true. Perhaps that's why, deep down inside herself, she believes she'll be a great teacher.

Like Elizabeth, her friend Dawn has grown to be an articulate, caring, and attractive young woman. Dawn Enjo has accepted her brother's move to Tokyo and, although she supports his efforts to

bring Japanese culture back into their family, she knows that her own focus is on her future here in Canada. She has strong artistic talents; a flair for design and decor. She has prepared for university, but has been assembling a portfolio for years and something is pulling her toward Art College.

Dawn's connection to Candace and Shawna Marie (another friend of Elizabeth's), remains strong, but her friendship with Elizabeth goes back to their early childhood and Dawn cherishes the bond between them. They have been and always will be there for each other. It's not something they have to say, they just know it.

*S*hawna Marie Verano's mother and dad emigrated from Argentina in the sixties. They moved first to Montreal, where she was born. Her mother read the name "Shawna" in a novel and combined it with "Marie." (Shawna Marie has yet to read the novel.) They then moved to southern Ontario where her dad found work in the steel mills. Shawna Marie became a regular in the strip the year that Elizabeth spent a summer on Bev and Dan's farm. Elizabeth came home to find that, in her absence, her best friend Dawn had become close to someone else. Elizabeth was jealous but tried to conceal her feelings. She eventually had to admit that matu-

rity means accepting new people into your circle of friends, and so Shawna Marie is often seen with Dawn and Elizabeth and others at the school, on the bus, in the pizza shop, and wherever this particular group of birds flocks. Shawna Marie is of medium-brown complexion, she has dark expressive eyes and a cloud of soft, back curly hair that bounces when she walks. She has a tiny diamond stud on the left side of her nose and a smile that could light up a stadium. She's athletic and good-natured and has decided to go into kinesthesiology . . . (now that she knows what it is).

Unlike Candace, she's predictable and positive, and Elizabeth's discovered that one can't have too many good friends.

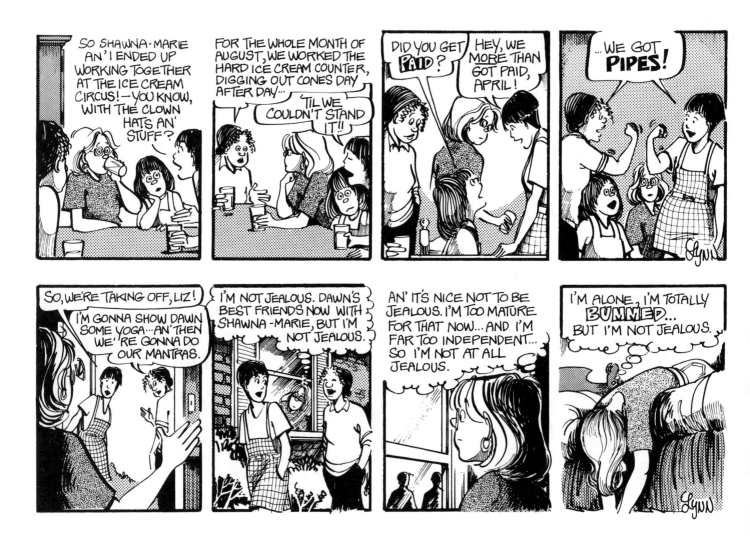

Over the years Candace Jessie Halloran has been on the ins and outs with Elizabeth. Either way, Liz has always imagined that Candace had a grip. Candace knew what was happening. Cool and full of attitude, she's always worn what "they" were wearing, talked the talk, and been opposed to just about everything.

When she shaved her head it was a gesture that said, Looks aren't everything. It was in opposition to what she'd always been and done, and, although not completely out of character, it was a radical change that her friends could not understand. What Dawn and Elizabeth didn't know about Candace was that when the bell rang and everyone gladly exited the school grounds, Candace never

went home. She would take any other route, any excuse, any delay to keep her away just a bit longer from a place she didn't want to be.

It was OK when she and her mom were on their own. Her mother was almost young enough to be her sister, having had her at the age of sixteen, but now her mom was living with a man Candace despised. She hated the way he looked at her and the way he touched her. She hated the way he lived in their apartment, using everything and contributing nothing.

There was always a reason for why he was unemployed. He had an injury or the job fell through or he was looking for something better. Candace's mother worked full-time at a shoe store, and on Thursdays and Fridays she came home late. Dawn and Elizabeth always wondered why she wanted to hang with them on these evenings; go someplace, take in a movie. They also wondered why, after all the times Candace had been invited to their homes, they were never invited to hers.

Candace shaved her head to make herself ugly. Not as a political statement but to make herself less appealing to her mother's boyfriend. He had been coming on to her more and more aggressively ever since she turned fifteen and he has let her know that it's only a matter of time before he hurts her. She now lives with friends.

Candace works evenings as a cashier in a corner store. She works as a waitress in the summer. Every cent she can save is put away for university, which she sees as her great escape. Her mother is helping her. This hard-working woman wants her daughter to have a good future, but Candace wonders why she's turned such a blind eye to the present and to the past.

Candace has had her ears pierced several times. She has four small tattoos. One of her closest friends is Duane Overfield, who is

also a familiar face in the school scenes. Duane's piercings, tattoos, and hair flair are legendary.

These two wild cards aren't as wild as they look. Bright and intelligent, there's an understanding between them that only a child who has suffered can share.

You can see by the annual rings on a tree when damage has been done. There are scars and signs of healing, and a specialist can tell you how and when these traumas occurred. Some people have annual rings, too. The pain of the piercing and the tattoos that Candace and Duane seem to need from time to time is a pain they control, a pain they can see and a pain they know will go away. Each pain comes with a badge of honor. Another stud, another ring, another tattoo; they are signs that one has chosen to be hurt and chosen to be healed. . . . something you can't do with spiritual wounds.

The message that these two will bring to their children is the knowledge that no matter how you were treated as a child, you are ultimately responsible for the way you treat others. Both have talked about careers in psychology. Both are good people. I hope they succeed.

HONK HONK!

HONK!

OFF TO THE BEACH?

YEAH! WE'VE GOT FOOD AN' EVERYTHING, MOM.

SOUNDS LIKE FUN! - CAN I COME?

SURE! WHY NOT!

THAT'D BE GREAT, MRS P.!

NO, I'M JUST KIDDING. I'VE GOT TOO MUCH TO DO HERE.

TOO BAD.

WHEW! THAT WAS CLOSE!

YEAH!

EVERY NOW AND THEN, I LIKE TO SHAKE THEM UP A LITTLE!

Lynn

*A*nthony Caine has been Elizabeth's friend for several years. I hesitate to say "boyfriend" because that's not exactly how she would describe him (although it's probably the way he would describe himself). His mother is Dutch, his dad British. They met and married in Canada. Anthony's tall and fair with reddish-blond hair and just a few freckles. He's worn glasses since he was seven and has never liked his nose. His voice changed late, his hands and feet grew before the rest of him did, and although he thinks he's got NERD written all over him, he's, well . . . not bad. In fact, he's the kind of kid that a girl's mother would point out. "See him? Wait twenty years and he'll knock the socks off any jock in the city! That's the kind of guy who's going to do well in whatever he chooses to do, and by golly—when he's got a little gray in his hair, he will be so handsome that every woman at your twentieth high school reunion will wonder why they didn't beg him to go out with them when they had the chance!" Mothers know these things. They've been to their own reunions and seen for themselves the nerd-to-knockout metamorphosis in the guys who were nobodies, while the jocks became jerks in the meantime.

But high school kids don't see this kind of potential in their peers...

and who's thinking that far into the future anyway? Anthony's future will include cars and computers and maybe a degree in Business Administration, but for now . . . he's just confused.

Anthony has been crazy about Elizabeth and he's hated her, too. He's wondered why they're still together. After all, she's had crushes on others and hasn't exactly told him she loved him. Not in actual words, anyway. But there's something that keeps them together. Maybe it's because what Elizabeth's brother, Michael once said is true: "Anthony's just like Dad."

> "Oh, yeah?!!! Oh, *really*?!!! Well, no way, José! You think I hang out with Anthony because he's like Dad? What kind of nutcase are you? JEEEESH!!! Oh, right! Sure! Like, I'd go 'round with somebody like my FATHER! THINK AGAIN, fish face, 'cause you are totally INSANE!!!"

After Elizabeth's unrepressed and animated response to his suggestion, Michael suspected he was right. And so do I. After all, I've been to my twentieth high school reunion. I know which nuts to pick.

There came a time in our lives when Rod and I wistfully considered the procreation of another child.

Kate was one and Aaron was five. We were well settled into the tiny northern mining community of Lynn Lake, and things seemed to be running smoothly enough for the bunch of us.

Then Aaron—who was not particularly enjoying school—led a walkout. He was in his senior year of kindergarten and, bored with *Mr. Bumpy and the Alphabet Train,* decided a change of scene was in order. Mid-reading, he stood up and said to his assembled classmates, "Who's not having any fun?" Hands went up. "Whoever's not having any fun, line up behind me." The teacher sat speechless as a line formed behind our son. "We're going out to play," he announced, and the parade marched through the door. The teacher headed them off in the hallway. "You can't do this!" she protested. Aaron explained, "We can, 'cause it's a vote. More people voted to go out and play than stay in." He was right. Most of the class was behind him. "So," he continued, "we win." The teacher sucked in her breath and then fired back with, "This is no democracy, young man. Go back to the classroom immediately!" Aaron countered with his automatic response to anything of a slightly disciplinary nature: "*It's no fair!!*"

Then our phone rang.

This wasn't the first time I'd sat in the school office, facing the accused, the accuser, and the principal. Although he was shaken by yet another encounter with the authorities, Aaron seemed to feel pretty comfortable with the whole scene. "So, here we are again," the conversation usually began . . . and would end with admonishments, promises, and a brisk walk home. Like me when I was a kid, Aaron was well liked by his teachers—as long as he wasn't in their class.

Aaron was not only a strong force to reckon with at school. He knew every trick in the book at home, too. We had ourselves a regular ball 'o' fire under our roof, and this meant that every neuron of adult intellect was needed in order to keep the peace. Or, a piece of it, anyway.

So the romantic notions I'd had of having another baby evaporated with the steam that regularly rose from our foreheads. Aaron took all the energy we had. Words my mother had once hissed at me came wafting back through space and time. "I'd have had more children if it wasn't for *you*!" I remembered her red face and bulging eyeballs and for some reason I'd felt a sense of accomplishment. I was six. It's hard to guess what a kid's really thinking, but I figured if I said this to Aaron, he was enough like me to consider it a compliment. So we just never had any more kids. It was a good thing.

This didn't mean that the thought was entirely eradicated. I'd see other young moms with bulging tummies or new babes and I'd go, "Awww."

I don't know why this happens. What is it that makes us forget stretch marks and backaches and labor pains and the (God help us all) episiotomy. This is a flowery word for something no man could or would ever imagine. You're in the middle of pushing something that feels like a wire coconut through a very delicate part of your anatomy and some idiot figures that a few snips of the scissors right there should give you some relief. Right!! Try sitting down afterward, sport! Try even walking! And don't even *consider* using the plumbing down there for any of the other things it's designed to do because the pain (they call it "discomfort") will fire you through a hospital washroom ceiling in two seconds flat. I'm surprised they don't install protective foam pads up there—but these guys aren't the ones who are suffering.

Then there's nursing. Now, I'm an advocate of breast feeding (the word "supporter" doesn't seem serious enough here), but the first few sessions of living with a high-powered suction device attached to something you don't even *scratch* too hard is a teeth clencher, for sure. At least it was for me. No loving photos have ever been taken of yours truly nursing a kid. Not a really small new one anyway. They're vicious. Later on, it gets easy. Even pleasurable. Well, anything that will pump you free of two pulsating footballs dangling from your sternum is welcome, believe me—and if this whole thing is nourishing, well, then, why not wait it out. I lasted six months with each kid. Some mothers let their three-year-olds

crawl under their shirts while they're having a latte in the mall—but not me. If it can walk, and especially if it has teeth, I'm done. But I had forgotten all this stuff along with the diapers, the all-nighters, the teething, toddling search-and-destroy days. I focused for a long time on how wonderful little kids really are, and during the day, when our kids were in school, I fantasized about having another one.

It wasn't until we'd moved from Lynn Lake to North Bay, Ontario, that I decided to introduce a new baby to the strip. I'd been in Los Angeles, visiting Cathy Guisewite, who does a comic strip called *Cathy* (if you're reading this, I'm sure you know her work). We had gone to visit a friend of hers who just had a baby boy. Cathy fidgeted for days trying to decide just what to take as a gift, so we'd been discussing kids, clothes, and comics for some time.

It often takes an outside observer to point out the obvious. "Why don't you just make one up?" she said. "Put a new baby in your strip!"

Until then, I'd rejected the idea because the characters had always been loosely based on us . . . but she had a point. I could go through pregnancy, have a baby, bring it home, and enjoy the good stuff all over again. I'd also be able to make fun of the bad stuff— which is very therapeutic, even when it's over.

Now, procreation by pen isn't as easy as you might think. First I had to come up with a conception date so that the new kid would arrive on April 1. This was important. Since this was a real fantasy, the birth had to happen on April Fool's Day.

Elly and John, surprisingly enough, managed to pull it off. This was followed by the announcement and the response, which would probably have been similar to our own family's response: "Are you *crazy*?!" Letters of congratulations came from readers who

genuinely believed we were *all* in the family way. We also got letters berating us for bringing yet another child into an already overpopulated world. We should have *adopted*! That's what they told us. I'm sure it was the same twits who sent letters of disgust when Farley, the cartoon family's dog, sired a litter with the lovely dog Sera next door. "You should have had that dog *neutered*!" The letters screamed. "How *dare* you advocate the indiscriminate breeding of neighborhood pets?!" (As far as I know, cartoons don't add too much pollution or take up a lot of space.)

Social commentary aside, the birth of April was an inspiring and thought-provoking bit of writing. Would Elly Patterson deliver at home or in the hospital? My obstetrician and dear friend Murray Enkin is one of the greatest advocates of modern midwifery. He has taught and written textbooks on the subject, and so when I asked him for advice, he naturally recommended that Elly and John prepare for a home birth. Elly was healthy, all was well. We even met with a group of midwives so that I'd understand more about their role in the event. Elly and I were ready for home birth. At that same time, however, controversy was brewing (controversy always brews).

During the early nineties, midwifery was beginning to emerge as a sensible, safe, and practical alternative to hospital delivery, which naturally forced the opponents of home birth to disagree vociferously. My own family doc was not in favor of home birth, and as the pros and cons were discussed in newspaper articles, call-in shows and hospital cafeterias, I began to realize that to have Elly Patterson deliver at home with the aid of a midwife would make a very political statement . . . and I was getting enough mail already. This is where storytelling becomes an art.

April Patterson was born at home by mistake! Remember how I told you about being able to control the weather? Well, when Elly went into labor, an ice storm just happened to make it impossible

for John to get home from work or for an ambulance to arrive. With the help of her neighbors, Carol Enjo (a nurse) and Connie Poirier (an X-ray technician), Elly Patterson safely delivered April Marian on April 1 (March 31 in the colored comics), saving me from the frustration of having to choose sides.

The really neat thing about April was, she seemed so real to me. I'd gone through the nine-month gestation with Elly (gaining some of the weight, even), and her birth was a genuine effort. I wasn't sure what she'd look like, but I hoped she'd look like Kate— and by golly, she did! Kate was born in 1977, three days after Christmas. Murray Enkin held her up and, with glee and affection,

said, "Lynn, you have a beautiful girl!" He then whisked us out of the hospital birthing room and hid us in a small room down the hall. Pulling a curtain around Rod and me and brand-new Katie, he whispered, "Get to know each other!" Kate's long dark hair was plastered to her forehead with the white chalky waters of birth. She was so instantly curious. Her dark blue eyes went from my face to Rod's. She looked around the room and back to us. Nobody can tell me that newborn babies can't see clearly and don't have questions to ask! We spent an hour with her alone, marveling at her—until a large nurse threw back the curtains and said, "She's *here*! We knew a baby had been born and we couldn't find her!" Then they took her away to be washed and weighed and . . . whatever.

Murray's gift to us of time alone with our brand-new baby will always be treasured. It was one of the most spiritual and meaningful times in our lives. No wonder he wished more parents could experience such privacy and intimacy. It's no wonder he is so loved.

Memories like this are nice to rekindle. April's birth was like having another baby, but without any "discomfort" or the hassle of preparing another room.

The family settled immediately into the new-baby routine, but the situation soon became more complicated by the arrival of John's cousin Fiona, who came (with her cat) to "help" the family out.

Where Fiona originated, I don't know. Well, I do know, but I'm not about to tell. Fiona is the friend or relative who arrives at your home to help out and . . . doesn't. They show up after births, deaths, major illnesses, and so on. The purchase of a new lakeside cottage brings them in droves. Their offer to help means they've brought beer and deck chairs so they can be comfortable while they cheer you on. Then they book the first two weeks in August. You know of whom I speak.

Elly and John were far too polite to turf out the abrasive and opinionated auntie. Fiona settled in with Belmont the cat the way raccoons infest an attic. Raccoons would have been preferable.

She was a great character. I had planned all sorts of frustratingly familiar tales of how one person's good intentions can be another's road to insanity. But Aunt Fiona and her cat were a little too much for the Pattersons and for the strip! With John's help, she moved to an apartment and became the manager of a small pool hall in town. The pool hall was to have been an irresistible magnet for Michael and his pals and play a consistent role, but it never happened. Fiona was too strong a character, introduced at a time

when the two older Patterson kids were doing and thinking adult stuff and the stories involving them were becoming longer and more detailed. Also, there was a new baby to focus on!

In my "other world," I know that Michael often visited Aunt Fiona—who eventually took over the pool hall—and Elizabeth too would haul off to "that part of town" whenever she felt defiant and wanted to run away.

As far as I know, Fiona is still running the pool hall, has had at least two major romances, still gambles, drinks, and smokes cigars, and wishes her cat hadn't run off. He probably didn't like her much, either.

Now, back to April! She was an easy baby to live with. She did all of the usual baby stuff, but by the time she was six months old, you knew that behind the innocent face was a mind full of pure mischief! Being much younger than Michael and Elizabeth was a plus for April. She knew she controlled the family. Darling one minute and devil the next, she explored, exposed, discovered, and dismembered everything she could reach, inside the house and out. She ate stuff the dog would have run from. She knew things they never expected her to know. She was trouble—and the best thing that had happened to the Pattersons in a long time.

Through April, I've had the fun of rediscovering everything from Santa Claus to superheroes. She's swallowed buttons and cut her hair, she's brought home fish and turtles and beetles and worms. She's made me kneel down and crawl under tables and bushes to see the world from her point of view and she's scared me half to death as well.

When April was born, Farley the family dog was getting on in years, but as I started to tell you before, he had enough spark in him to accept an invitation from the dog next door; and this encounter resulted in the arrival of his son, Edgar. The Pattersons did the right thing and happily adopted the new puppy, thus complicating their lives and my story lines even more.

By the time Edgar was as big as his dad, April was tall enough to reach the latch on the back gate. One spring day when the water in the creek behind the house was running high, April found a toy boat and, accompanied by the two dogs, decided to go down into the ravine and see if it was seaworthy. John's mother was staying with the family, and when she heard Edgar's insistent barking, she knew something was wrong. John, his mother, Elly, and Elizabeth ran down to the creek to find Farley holding April's head above water and using every ounce of his strength to do so.

It was a hard series to write and even harder to draw. The rescue part of the story lasted several days. With the dog's help, John managed to pull April out of the water, but for Farley the effort had been too much. He was weak with exhaustion and died in Elizabeth's arms.

It was a really sad story. It was scary and it was sad.

I thought about it for a year before I wrote the story. Then I wrote slowly and thoughtfully. Farley was an old dog, and if I was going to be true to the strip, he had to live out his life in real time. It was a story I desperately did not want to write. When I told Charles Schulz what I planned to do, he was actually quite mad at

me. "You cannot kill off the family dog!" he said straight out. "If you do that, I'll have Snoopy hit by a truck and go to the hospital and everyone will worry about Snoopy and won't read about poor Farley." So I didn't tell him when the story would run. Only my husband and my editor knew.

When I'd finished writing the four-week episode, I drew it in pencil and took it to the workshop to show Rod. He wiped the sawdust from his hands and carefully handled the panels. I watched his eyes fill with tears as he read the story. "I can't believe Farley's going to die," he said. "Do you really have to do this?" I believed in my heart that I did.

Farley went a hero. As the drama unfolded, the letters came. People told me they'd sat on the subway and cried. Many letters were angry; others, objective and understanding. I received photos of pets and cards of sympathy, but the most amazing response of all came from a man who sent me a beautiful granite tombstone that read, FARLEY, OUR HERO 1981–1995. A perfect likeness of him was engraved next to the words. It lies in our garden in a small private spot where Willy, our little black spaniel, is buried. People who see the two stones stop and think about the two dogs. In so many ways, one was as real as the other, and both are very sadly missed.

Very unfortunately, when the story ran, something awful happened. Farley died during the Oklahoma City bombing. I could never have known, when I'd sent my work in eight weeks before, that millions of people would soon be overwhelmed with grief, and that this was a story they didn't need to see at this time.

Some people used Farley's story to teach their children about death. Some told me it brought back memories of their own heroic animals. We received and responded to over a thousand letters. In Edmonton, the spring runoff had filled the rivers to overflowing, and one of the schools used the story to teach youngsters about the danger in playing near fast-running water. I hoped, as my phone rang and the mail arrived, that perhaps somewhere some little one April's age had escaped tragedy because of it.

Farley's disappearance from the strip was a natural passage. It happened five years ago now, and people still tell me they remember Farley the dog, how he lost his life, and how it touched them. This and the story about Lawrence are, to date, the most remembered of my small explorations into the serious side of life.

One thing I neglected to do when Farley died (and this was firmly pointed out to me by several readers) was to acknowledge the heroic role Edgar had played in the drama. If he hadn't been smart enough to run up the hill and bark for help, nobody would have known that April and Farley were in trouble.

This wasn't an oversight. I just didn't have enough space or time to tell the story in such detail.

April grew up by a visible notch after the rescue, and Edgar went from being a doofus to a dog with character.

Edgar has his father's sheepdog looks, and he has his mother's ears, nose, and coloring. It's taken time, but he's now accepted as being the Patterson family's dog. I found it hard, too, to get used to him, but he's family now. I think of his character as being a lot like

Don Knotts . . . and I absolutely *love* to draw him!

April has just turned eight years old. She's fun to write about and delightful to be. April is Katie and Aaron and me. She's also a lively spirit unto herself. She loves pets of all kinds and dreams about horses. She skates and swims and wants to be able to travel anywhere, just by closing her eyes. She has two close friends, Becky McGuire, a slender child with curly blond hair and a great imagination, and Duncan Anderson, whose family came from Barbados. Duncan's background includes British rugby, schools with uniforms, island festivals, and Caribbean sun. He speaks with just a hint of an accent, and he loves pets and baseball and computer games that take you into space. Becky and April quarrel sometimes, but they have much in common. As an only child, Becky identifies with April. They play well together, and Elly knows that when Elizabeth goes away to university April will need her friends more than ever.

For now, though, she loves her school and her pets, her friends and her family. She's a joy to her parents and accepts each day as a brand-new adventure. Elly and John have produced a journalist and perhaps a teacher! What's next? They're beginning to view the zoo in the basement through different lenses. Could it be

that the little girl who brings home injured birds, baby toads, and earthworms is just practicing? April once said she'd like to work with animals. Maybe, someday, she will.

*U*ncle Phil was the first family member outside the Patterson household to become a familiar face in *For Better or For Worse*. I needed no imagination here; I just based Elly Patterson's brother on my own—who is himself a character. Alan Ridgway is an excellent musician, creative storyteller, capable fix-it guy, wine enthusiast, traveler, and one of those teachers I talked about who teaches from the heart. He's one of the most entertaining people I know. He has a natural sense for comic timing, for the right words to describe things, and for expressions that need no words at all. He's always been funny, and maybe that's another reason I was so jealous of him when we were kids.

I was living in southern Ontario as a single mom when Alan decided to leave Vancouver and seek his musical fortunes in the great East. He arrived on the doorstep of my tiny house carrying his suitcase, his trumpet, a music stand, and laundry.

Over a shared beer, we discussed his evident *state of lost*. The house had two bedrooms and Aaron, just a baby, needed one of them. There was no basement, so when Alan moved in he accepted the garage as his headquarters. In the beginning he worked at a screen door factory during the day and as a musician at night, coming home to a folding bed next to the lawnmower. He was the kind of guy who could make do and did.

He formed a brass quintet, gave private lessons, and worked at the Stratford Festival Theatre—but the need for more stability in his life sent him back to British Columbia for a teaching degree. He now teaches music in a progressive high school in southern

Ontario, and we reminisce about the months he lived in my garage, shaking our heads with, "Remember when?"

Uncle Phil just walked into the strip one day and made himself at home. Slapstick, single, and sarcastic, his sister wondered if he would be a good influence on the children . . . and the children naturally hoped he would not.

It was Uncle Phil who introduced young Michael to the art of babe watching, to the combined effects of rotgut and roller coasters (rotgut being a mixed assortment of fairground soft drinks). He smoked, drank beer, and considered a good meal to be red meat with maybe a spud. Fry the spud and it became food-like. Green stuff was poison. The kids adored him.

Elly soon introduced her brother, Phil, to Connie Poirier next door, and the two began seeing each other. I have to break away a little here and tell you that when Phil started dating Connie, a single mother, my brother, started dating a young woman who had a child. The coincidence was interesting; he called to tell me. "How did you know?" I didn't.

Connie and Phil's relationship was never clearly defined in the strip, so I suspect they never really knew what attracted them to each other—except that Connie loved music, and there was music and mischief wherever Phil went. He moved to an apartment and traveled a great deal, taking jobs in Ottawa, Kingston, and Montreal. He loved Connie, but his dedication to his art and the

sometimes long separations between them made Connie wonder if they could make a go of it. She hadn't quite disarmed the defense system she'd built since her divorce.

Phil came back from a gig to find that Connie had met and had started going out with Ted McCaulay. It was bad news. He brought his grievances to his sister and consoled himself with the cigarettes he was trying hard to give up.

Here I have a mental image of my brother one cold and windy Thanksgiving. A fine, freezing rain had begun to fall. We had just finished dinner and were relaxing with another glass of wine, and Alan, still addicted to the weed, needed to light up. We asked him to go outside and he did so without hesitation, but he stood at the window, his shoulder against the frame of the house. His wool cap was pulled down to his eyebrows, the collar of his jacket was pushed up to his ears, and he smoked, holding the butt between shivering lips. He inhaled slowly, then dropped his jaw to let the smoke escape with the steam. He looked like a miserable stray dog banished to suffer in the elements, while we sat comfortably inside. He played it to the hilt. Alan is good.

So Uncle Phil went on with his career and eventually met a lovely young woman called Georgia. She was intelligent and attractive and slender with dark hair, green eyes, and a happy disposition.

I had wanted to call her Jane. I don't know why: the name and the J-sound were right. John's receptionist, however was Jean—so with John and Jean already in the strip, a Jane could have been confusing. I called Phil's new love Georgia, thinking it would be shortened affectionately to Geo from time to time.

Meanwhile, my brother—in real life—had broken up with the woman he'd been seeing (the single mom) and had met a wonderful young woman who was intelligent, attractive, and slender, with dark hair, green eyes, and a happy disposition. *Her* name was Joan.

It was another interesting coincidence—so interesting, in fact that he called me and said, "Sis, stop predicting my life—and oh, by the way, I'm going to ask Joan to marry me, so you'd better not have Phil ask Georgia to marry him first!"

Alan and Joan were married. It was a beautiful wedding. Phil and Georgia were married soon after.

Phil settled down with Georgia. He'd been the sort of spontaneous, carefree, and unpredictable character you could bring into the picture at any time; now he was a married man, settled into a suburban home and working regular hours, teaching music at a school. I was never able to explain how he got the job or what Georgia did, but I always meant to. With Phil and Georgia Richards in their new home, I went back to the other characters, knowing I would return to them in time and pick up where I left off.

So much was happening. I followed one new story line after another, leaving Phil and Georgia to continue their lives undocumented. It wasn't until Grandma Marian's illness a couple of years later that Phil came back into the strip.

This has happened to a number of favorite characters: Aunt Fiona is one, Sharon Edwards is another, and then there is Annie! There are so many stories I want to tell and plan to tell . . ..

While Phil and Georgia were left to deal with some difficult neighbors, Elly was working at a new job, April was active and meeting new kids, Mike and Elizabeth had adult relationships, and Gordon got married . . ..

Elly's husband, John, was also left somewhat out of the picture. He came home and interacted with the family, but other than that he had no life. I knew where he was and what he was doing, but nobody else did. Whole sequences of him at work, arguing with Ted, dealing with his own personal stuff, were noted down but never drawn. I just didn't have time. Generally, ideas for comic strips are hard to come by. I've always had the opposite problem!

So, for all of you who've asked me, Phil and Georgia still live in the land of *For Better or For Worse*. Phil accepted a teaching position in Montreal last year and they were uprooted from their home near Elly and John. Georgia works with developmentally challenged kids, Phil teaches during the day, and in the evenings he plays jazz with a group of musicians who play for the joy of it. They have no children but are, in their own way, mentors to many.

The Pattersons see them as often as possible. Elizabeth sings to the accompaniment of her Uncle Phil's guitar and April watches, wondering if it's an instrument she could play some day. Then there'd be "real" music all the time.Elly enjoys her brother's company. They've gotten to know each other better since they both passed forty. The death of their mother and concerns about their dad have made them closer. Will you see Phil and Georgia again? Absolutely! They are wonderful characters, and if Phil and Elly are a lot like Alan and me, it's on purpose. After all these years, I still love teasing my little brother.

Alan and Joan have allowed me to capture just a small part of the joy and the humor and the creativity that is them, and I thank them with all my heart!

When Michael Patterson went to his first college lecture, Josef Myron Weeder sat next to him. His hair wasn't quite as wild as it is now, and his nose didn't appear to be as large, but it was Weed just the same. I recognized him from art school in the sixties, from campus rallies on TV, from crowded bars and experimental theatre. He stands out in a crowd. Like Candace and Duane, he wears a costume, but perhaps not one so difficult to see through.

Jo—or Weed, as everyone calls him—has been Michael Patterson's closest friend for the past five years. Their relationship has survived a bawdy life in residence, closely shared living space, and . . . Mrs. Dingle.

They've traveled and studied and worked together. In so doing, they have discovered that Jo's talent as a photographer and Michael's ability to write can be artfully combined to form a viable and exciting business partnership. They're a team.

Weed is outgoing and outrageous; he's willing to do anything for a laugh. He's motivated and hard-working and focused on his career. His tinted glasses keep you from seeing directly into his eyes, and so you never really make contact with this funny but intense young man. Despite the number of hours he and Michael have spent together at home and on the road, he has divulged surprisingly little about himself. Michael has often wondered why Weed has never really talked about his parents or invited him home.

Josef Myron Weeder is the only son of a prominent businessman. His sister, Charlotte, is a nurse, single and working in the States. His mother, Eva, is a socialite whose entire life has been devoted to creating the perfect home and acquiring the perfect friendships. Jo senior is an importer of fine textiles and has traveled the globe many times. Ironically, Annie Nichols's husband, Steve, is one of his salesmen. (Annie and Steve live next to the Pattersons, it's a small world!) Mr. Weeder has a number of other business interests as well—some he records diligently, some he does not. All involve importing, all have made him supremely wealthy. Their Rosedale house is an enormous multichambered Tudor place that to Weed is more like a mausoleum than a family home. Richly decorated with elegant and expensive furnishings, every room has the ambiance of acquisition. Even the kitchen appears to have been taken from *Mansions* magazine. The brass pots, spoons, and strainers hanging from the wrought iron hook rail over the center island appear to have never been used.

Light filters through leaded glass, whose beveled edges look

like gemstones, set into the plush burgundy and emerald window dressings. The rooms are dark despite the many alcoves, French doors, and casements that let in the sun. There is a smell of old wood and silver polish. Even a well-balanced bouquet of fresh flowers in the "entertainment" room fails to make one feel at ease. Joseph Weeder's parents' house is a symbol of what they've earned and what they own, and nothing here, he feels, belongs to him.

For years, the Weeders had been preparing their son to take over the family business. He had traveled with his father many times, to Russia and Turkey and Italy and Greece. He had been enrolled in private schools, and in the summertime he worked in the shipping rooms at the warehouse in Toronto—"something to build character," his dad said. "Teach him the business from the ground up."

When he graduated from grade school, he was told that he would get a degree in business and join the firm. Josef was eighteen when he left for the University of Toronto. He never arrived for his first class.

Josef Weeder got a job in a photography shop on Bay Street and learned everything he could about cameras and lighting, composition, and design. He read books and he assisted professional photographers for free, just to watch how they did things. He watched and he remembered and he knew he was where he belonged.

He told his parents that his first year in university was going fine. He knew they'd believe him. He was safe. Throughout his life, they had been consistent. They had missed his soccer games, his first play, and his high school graduation. His marks were what was important. Like a stock market analyst, his dad would scan his documents for numbers up, numbers down, percentage remarks and totals. They had never really taken an interest in *him*, in what he wanted to do, so he knew that for a year at least he would be safe in his deception.

He lived in a small flat with a shared bathroom and kitchen. He was consumed by his work. By spring he had enough samples in his portfolio to apply to the college in London, Ontario, to the department of Photography and Design. By summer, he had been accepted, and by then he had the courage to tell his parents what he had done.

To his immense relief and surprise, their response was more disappointment than anger. He was young, they reasoned. He needed to experiment. They decided to allow their son to complete his course at the college, believing that in time he would come to see

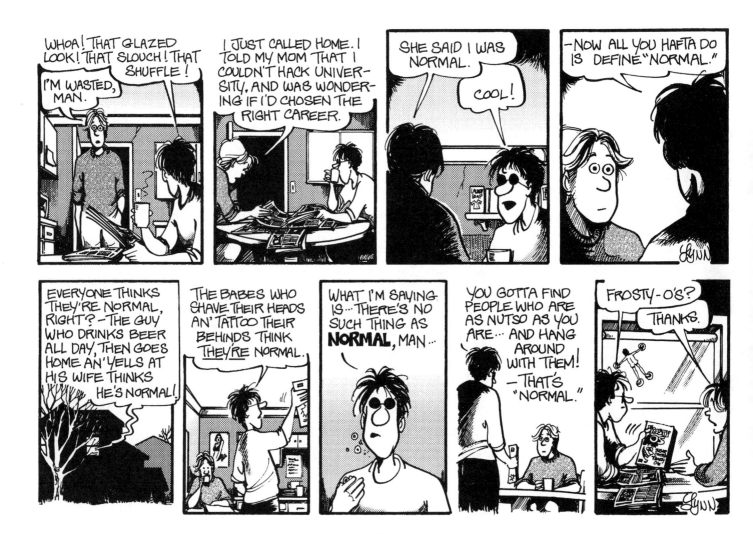

that a business degree and the "gift" of their empire was his only sensible goal. He had saved money from working, but he still needed help to survive. They agreed to support him, which was a concession he never expected. Perhaps behind their aggressiveness and control there was compassion and understanding. But it came too late. Jo had already sealed himself off from them, and he sealed himself off from others as well. For Josef Weeder it's always been easier to go solo, to depend on the one person who would be there for him unconditionally. Still, it's hard to rely on yourself for everything.

Josef Weeder has allowed Michael Patterson into his world enough to believe in his friendship and trust his ability. He knows that together they have the potential to do good things. He has stopped looking for his parents' approval because he genuinely approves of himself, and come what may the fortune they have amassed is theirs to do with as they see fit. His fortunes are personal and out there, waiting.

Waiting also is someone with whom he'll share his life. He isn't yet ready to risk the roller coaster of romance, but he thinks about it. He's about to shed his tinted glasses for clear ones. He just has to clear his mind, first.

Michael Patterson and Deanna Sobinski met by accident. While driving home from school one weekend, Deanna fell asleep at the wheel. Her car went through a guard rail and rolled down an embankment on the side of the highway. Michael and Weed saw the accident and were the first to arrive on the scene.

Being journalists, they saw a story in Deanna's twisted car. They took pictures and notes as two truck drivers pulled her from the wreck. So eager were they to get their article and photos to the local paper, the two boys overlooked the fact that they had used a near tragedy to boost their marks—without thought for the victim,

without the presence of mind to help.

Later, filled with guilt and remorse, Michael went to the hospital to apologize to the young woman he had written about—and, strangely enough—he knew her! Deanna Sobinski, the same little girl who had moved away so many years ago, the little girl he'd teased and adored in elementary school, the one he had missed so much, was looking at him from a hospital bed and forgiving him for being human.

This story was based on something that actually happened to us. Our son, Aaron, was working for a local television station. He had been given a camera and a company car and was to drive to

the lakeshore to take some shots of the sunset over which they planned to superimpose the typed weather forecast, after the news. On his way, he heard a police message on the car's CPIC [Canadian Police Information Center] radio. There was an accident and he was excited. He knew he would be the first and perhaps the only news cameraman at the scene. He arrived as the police and the ambulance did and taped the awful wreckage of a small sedan, overturned in a ditch. The young woman inside had not survived. He continued to film despite protests from the attending paramedics and raced home to tell us that his work would be on the evening news, that the shots he got were "fantastic," and wouldn't it be great if they went national? We watched the news. "They didn't use the best part of my footage," he said, as we watched the awful scene . . . and then they gave the name of the victim. It was a girl he knew well. His hands shook, his face went white, and he cried.

Aaron attended his friend's funeral, and grieved with her family. She was so young. He came home and promised, "For the rest of my life I will never again see anything like this without first thinking about the people involved. I will never again be so insensitive." It was a terrible way to learn an important lesson.

So Deanna's accident was one of the few stories I've done that was generated by a true and very personal event.

Deanna is the younger of Wilfred and Mira Sobinski's two daughters. Her older sister is a lawyer, newly married and living in Halifax. The Sobinskis are third-generation Canadian; their family emigrated from Poland in the late 1800s. They still speak a little Polish at home and Mrs. Sobinski continues to make the same dishes from the same recipes her grandmother used.

They're proud of their daughter and approve of her friends—but they still embarrass her sometimes, the way they did when she was fifteen. Deanna begs her dad not to tease and interrogate the boys she brings home. "But that's my job," he's fond of saying, and I guess in some ways it is.

Deanna is twenty-three, and about to graduate with a degree in pharmacy from the University of Western Ontario. It hasn't been an easy five years. Despite her intellect and her efforts, she has had to redo several of her courses, and the sheer volume of information she had to learn often left her reeling with exhaustion and questioning her career choice again and again.

She was always an easygoing kid, interested in music and softball and movies and friends. She has a pretty face, and light blond hair and she speaks with a slight and endearing *th* when she says the letter *s*. She looks fragile, but her strength is in her character and in her convictions to give back something to the world she feels has given so much to her.

Deanna Sobinski genuinely loves Michael Patterson, but she is not prepared to marry, not yet. When she broke her engagement to a boy she'd known in high school, she vowed that the next time she made such a promise, it would be after she had achieved something for herself, something that would define who she was and what she was.

Deanna has decided to go to Honduras after she graduates.

It's an opportunity to use what she's learned in school while she learns something about life. She'll be working with a medical team in an area where there are no pharmacies, no drugs, none of the health resources we so easily take for granted here. She knows she'll return a different person in many ways, and Michael hopes she'll stay the same.

They're a good team and they know it. They also know they will have to let each other go from time to time.

I've had many letters from people who ask, "When are Michael and Deanna going to get married?" Well, the answer is, "I don't know. They're young, they have plenty of time and like their parents . . . I think it should be their own decision."

$\mathcal{T}$he landlady from Hell. That's what I wanted Mrs. Dingle to be. Miserly, miserable, and perpetually focused on everyone else's business, she was going to be someone you love to hate, but she became someone you hate to love—or at least can't help liking, just a little.

When Mike and Weed left residence and moved into the small frame bungalow on Cleveland Street, they shared the main and upper floors with two female students, and the landlady lived in the basement. (The evil, down below.)

The girls were fun and full of potential but, again, I had

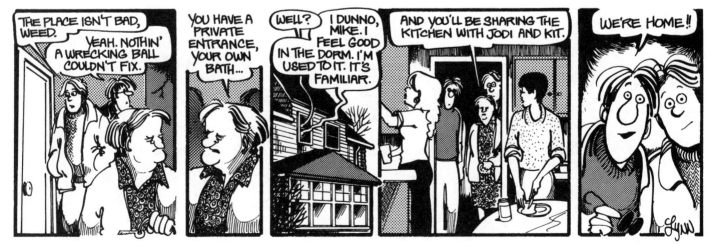

weighed myself down with too many characters, so Jody and Kit moved out. Mrs. Dingle relocated to the main floor and Michael and Weed controlled the upstairs, which consists of two bedrooms, kitchen, "wreck room," and can.

I don't know what it is about eye bags and hair rollers, but I love to draw them. Often toothless and dressed in shapeless frocks, Agnes Dingle patrols the premises. With her ear to the wall and her eyes peeled, she looks like something you'd find in a cave somewhere under a rock. But then . . . you shine a light on her and she glows a little.

The problem with putting an ugly stereotype into a lifelike situation is that people aren't all bad. Sooner or later, you get to know something about them, and you figure out why they are the way they are. Then the evil spell is broken and you feel some empathy and even affection for these sometimes deservedly lonely people.

On a whim one evening, Mike and Weed invited their landlady to share a beer with them at the local watering hole, the Bung and Wattle; a place where water is only consumed when one's stomach contents need to be diluted . . . or else. They toasted Weed's top marks for a photo essay. They even danced a little and learned that their landlady had a life.

Agnes Dingle grew up in the south of England. Poor and uneducated, she left her family and moved to Canada at the age of eighteen. She married a Saskatchewan farmer, a man she had met through correspondence. They had three children and lived a hard life, working the land, selling what they could, consuming what was left over. Bobby Dingle was a drinker who loved to play darts in the evening and often came home minus the money he'd kept for supplies. She ran the household and much of the farm on her own. Her children, two sons and a daughter, managed the heavy work outside. Bobby was "one more kid," but he worked hard when he was sober and he loved her. That's all that mattered.

When the kids were finally grown and gone, the load and the loans became impossible. They filed for bankruptcy, and almost everything they owned was sold at auction. Bobby Dingle was now a fixture at the bar. Agnes decided to take what little money she had hidden away and move to London, Ontario, where her elder son was settled with a job and a family. She sold her rings and her mother's cedar chest and paid two months' rent on the small house on Cleveland Street. It had extra rooms. She could rent some of them to students.

Her husband was emotionally unable to make the move. With his drinking severe and his health compromised, he was admitted to a chronic care facility, where he died soon afterward.

Bitter and isolated, Agnes has been living alone and in the past. She trusts few people, sees one of her sons only on holidays, and generally keeps herself separated from the noisy and energetic kids who rent her rooms upstairs. She watches them, though, and listens, and she wishes she had it all to live over again. She'd do a lot of things differently. But when she sees his photo on the mantel and remembers the good times, she knows she'd marry Bobby Dingle all over again and make the best of it.

Mrs. Dingle has been a wonderful character. When you bring someone like this to life, you imagine yourself in her shoes; you try to think and to feel and to behave the way she would. It's an acting job, I guess—and yet, there she is in black and white, real enough to look at and care about, real enough to have lived a life, real enough to exist.

Michael and Weed will be going into partnership together, which means they'll need more space to work and to live in. They'll need to be closer to Toronto and to the airport. Neither of them wants to leave the small house on Cleveland Street that has been home for so long, and they know they'll miss Mrs. Dingle.

Agnes Dingle hasn't said much. She watches Michael preparing for graduation and Josef Weeder scanning the *Toronto Star*'s "to rent" section, but she keeps her feelings to herself. In her life, she has lost too many things. Why allow yourself to become attached to people when, in the end, they go away?

What she doesn't know is that Mike and Weed see in her a story that is worth writing about. No matter where their future takes them, no matter how their lives evolve, they know they'll never forget her. Mrs. Dingle is one of a kind. They plan to keep in touch.

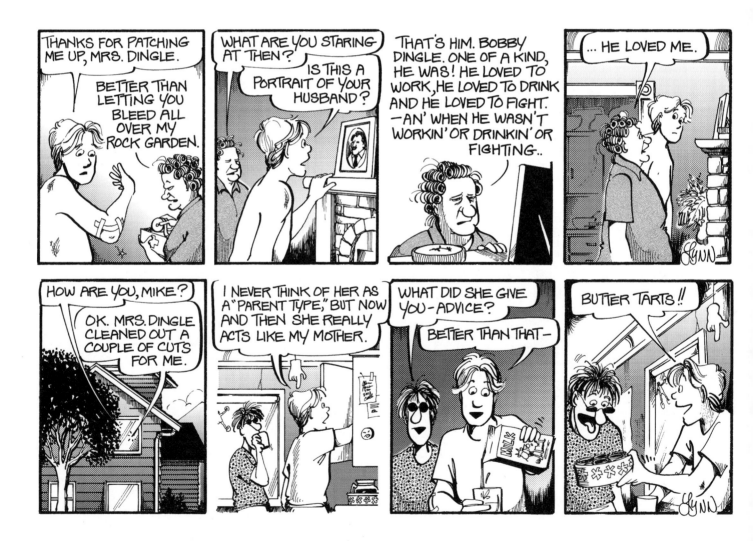

*B*ack again in time. It was 1977. Rod and I were just married and living in Dundas, Ontario. Aaron was four, I was working freelance from a studio in our greenhouse, and Rod, who was then in his second year of dental school, was looking for a summer job. I had three small cartoon books published, but the income from them was minimal, and commercial art business was not streaming my way. We were living "carefully." (When roadkill looks good, you worry.)

Rod's sister, Beth, then a veterinarian, lived (and still lives) with her husband, Don, on a farm just south of Winnipeg, Manitoba. They needed some help that summer and offered us four months' work. Loaded with kid and kaboodle, we headed our car west and rolled into their driveway just as Beth, a tall attractive woman, was leaving the house, dressed in coveralls and carrying a toolbox. She was about to castrate fifty pigs. I bounced out of the car in my matching pink shirt, shorts, and sneakers and offered to help. Beth looked at me with one of her "What do we have here?" sort of looks and handed me a pair of boots and her other set of coveralls. Together we caught, sexed, castrated, and vaccinated fifty pigs. It was hard work and dirty—but surprisingly fast. (Castration, interestingly, is really quite simple. For the rest of the day, we were called "castrating women!") That was my first introduction to life on the farm—and Beth said I passed.

We worked from May to September. Rod and Don built a pig barn, put up grain bins, and worked on the tractors out in the fields. I cooked and cleaned and helped Beth in her veterinary clinic. It was such a busy time. There were no other children on the farm, and Aaron was in constant danger of getting hurt. Ruth and Tom Johnston, Rod's mom and dad, came down from the north to look after him, and they were wonderful.

Those months in Manitoba changed me so much. They introduced a city kid to the life-and-death, matter-of-fact business of running a farm. It wasn't something I instantly took a shine to, either. I went from eager beaver to pain-in-the-arse and back again. I learned to drive a combine, to look up and see a prairie storm coming from miles away, to appreciate where food comes from and how hard it is to grow. There is no one more innovative, patient, or business savvy than a farmer!

The farm is where you learn to make things yourself, to rely on each other, and to accept the fact that dirt will enter your house through every portal no matter what you do, so live with it and

clean up when it rains.

I have to thank my husband and his family for so many things, but most of all for this education.

Beth and Don Cruikshank had to be in the strip. They are spontaneously funny. They are storytellers, creative and intellectual and artistic. I never asked them first, I just hoped they'd go along with it, and they did, so far without reprisal.

Rod's mom and dad also appear quite often. It's so much easier to caricature people and places that really exist. Sadly, Ruth and Tom have passed away, but we keep their memory alive through the strip.

Beth and Don became Bev and Dan. Rod's parents became Grandma Carrie and Grandpa Will (their second names). For reference, I use old photographs of Beth and Don's house and a big family portrait that shows all of us together. Since the Pattersons had children, I wanted there to be a cousin on the farm to play with and so the cartoon Bev and Dan have a daughter, Laura. She is the same age as Elizabeth, and she's neat.

Here again is where both *our* lives and the lives of the characters in the strip intertwine and become complicated. In real life, Beth and Don Cruikshank have three beautiful daughters; Lauren, Christine, and Arli. Lauren, the eldest, is Kate's age, and when the

four girls get together, they have a wonderful time. Although Chris and Arli have never come right out and asked me why there's only one cousin in the strip, I know they wonder. It's because I couldn't write for three cousins. I could only work comfortably with one! With four panels and one statement a day, you can only explore a make-believe world so far. So Laura is in fact an amalgamation of three beautiful girls whom their Auntie Lynn thinks the world of. Here is a sincere thanks to them and to my sister and brother-in-law, for being so easy to draw and draw *from*.

We miss Rod's mom and dad terribly. Rod's dad was the mill superintendent in a copper mine; his mom was a teacher and a weaver.

For many years they lived close to us, a ten-minute walk away, and now they live on in the strip. I imagine Grandma Carrie and Grandpa Will Patterson to be retired farmers. Having sold their farm to Bev and Danny, they now live in the small Manitoba town they've been so much a part of all their lives. They enjoy driving the long country roads in the summertime, checking crops and visiting neighbors. Bev and Dan see them often. They are a joyful and generous pair—and still in love. Whenever I draw them it's like tracing the faces of Ruth and Tom. It's a good feeling, and part of what makes this job so enjoyable.

I've put my brother Alan and Rod's sister Beth into *For Better or For Worse*, but Rod's brother has never been represented in cartoon form. I asked Ralph Johnston recently if he felt left out and he said no. He told me he always believed he was Lawrence, and in fact Lawrence at twenty-four looks a little like Ralph when I first met him.

It's nice to know that he considers himself part of all this, because he is. If I were to try and draw my brother-in-law as he really is, I would need a separate strip altogether. In fact Rod and Ralph and Beth could provide enough material to sustain a comedy network for years.

I definitely married into the right family.

WOULD YOU LIKE A LITTLE MORE, DAD?

NO, THANKS, DEAR.

MY SUFFICIENCY HAS BEEN SUFFANC-IFIED, AND MORE WOULD BE SUPER-FLUOUS!

YOU MADE ANOTHER FINE MEAL, ELLY.

THANKS, DAD.

REMEMBER THE HOLIDAY DINNERS WE HAD WHEN YOU WERE LITTLE?

MM-HMM.

MY, THEY WERE FUN! - BUT YOU KNOW WHAT THE BEST PART WAS?...

AFTER THE TABLE WAS CLEARED, THERE WAS ONE THING THAT ALWAYS BROUGHT US TOGETHER AS A FAMILY.

AND...THANKS TO A TWIST OF FATE, HERE WE ARE TO-NIGHT!

WHAT'S GOING ON?

THE DISHWASHER'S BROKEN.

I was watching a building burn down last summer when a complete stranger walked up to me and said, "You Lynn Johnston?" Yes, I said. "You Merv Ridgway's daughter?" That's me, I said. "Well," he continued, after a long drag on his cigarette, "we're related."

I knew he was right. I could tell by the bulb on his nose that he was somebody from Dad's side of the family. I figured he might want to talk. You know, reminisce about somebody or something that might connect us socially, but having confirmed that we were indeed from the same gene pool, he turned and walked back toward the burning building for a better look.

I've met a number of familial offshoots in this manner. The nose does it every time.

My dad, Mervyn Ridgway, was quite a character. He loved to sing and play the guitar and he never forgot a joke. Not even the groaners. Mom—Ursula—was far more conservative, and together they made an odd but very devoted couple. They were the kind of people who could make or do anything and will always be remembered by their friends and neighbors as generous people, kind to everyone and fun to have around.

They're gone now, too. I look at the photos on my studio wall and find it hard to believe that I can't call them up and say hi. Not on the phone, anyway.

Grandpa Jim and Grandma Marian in the strip are so closely based on my parents that I hear their voices when I draw them. I see them in three dimensions. They walk into my mind as if they had walked through our front door, and when I write their lines they seem to be writing them for me. I imagine Grandpa Jim to be a retired gift shop owner who loved to chat with his customers and slip in the occasional "something for the kids" for free. He still goes down to the old place and talks to the man who took her over. There are several boxes in the downstairs storage room and only he knows what's inside. He loves to sit in the corner coffee shop and sneak a cigarette. If Grandma Marian can't see him smoking, she can't pressure him to quit.

I imagine that Grandma Marian was a stenographer and a bookkeeper, skills she learned during the war. I imagine that she met and married Jim when he came home from England, his air-force uniform dark beside the white cotton dress she wore on their wedding day. I imagine the lives of Jim and Marian Richards. They are quite similar to the lives of Merv and Ursula Ridgway, a watch-

HOW LONG ARE YOU GOING TO STAY WITH US, GRAMPA?

PUT IT THIS WAY.... AS LONG AS I'M NEEDED.

WHAT ARE YOU DOING, APRIL?

LOOKING FOR SOMETHING TO BREAK.

Lynn

maker and a calligrapher. Sometimes it's difficult to separate the real from the fantasy. Sometimes I don't want to.

Mom died of cancer eight years ago. It was a long process and she took on the challenge with courage and ingenuity. What's interesting is that she analyzed her feelings and her progress both from a clinical and from a spiritual point of view. She wanted to explore this passage like a researcher, questioning, learning, accepting, and sharing every part of it. It was a privilege to be with her at this time, and because she would have wanted me to, I told her story in the strip.

It was strangely comforting for me to do so, and through the

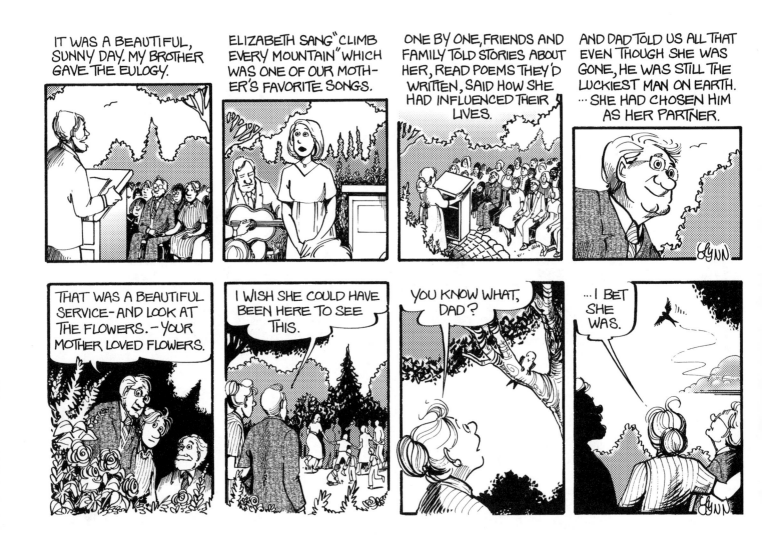

many letters I received, I discovered that it was a story that comforted others as well.

What we didn't know when Mom died was that Dad was seriously ill, too. For over a year, he nursed Mom at home, focusing all his attention on her. He rarely left her side, and when she died, he died too, in a way. A short while later, my brother Alan and I were placing a second stone in the small military cemetery near the home they so loved in British Columbia.

We had hoped Dad would come to live here with us. He had been born and raised in Ontario and it seemed like a natural transition. Things rarely happen the way you plan them in real life; Dad died before we could arrange for him to move. But, Grandpa Jim was alive and well in the strip, and there was a chance that he'd accept Elly and John's offer to move in with them. He did so, for a while, but he felt more at home in the little retirement home he'd bought with Marian in Vancouver.

He's come back to visit. He even has a pretty Sheltie dog companion. Her name is Dixie, and she's a lot like the dog my dad always wanted to have.

As time goes by, Jim may change his mind and move in with his daughter. Elizabeth is going to university soon, there'll be another empty room in the house on Sharon Park Drive . . . and little April loves her grandpa.

As long as Jim Richards lives on in the strip, a little bit of home lives on for me. I draw Grandpa Jim from a photograph of my parents, and when I draw him I draw my dad—and for some reason I always start with his nose.

When it comes to mixing up real people with the fictitious ones, Elly and John and Rod and I become the most confused. If this whole thing confuses us, it most definitely confuses everyone else, so trying to say who is who and when would be a tedious exercise and I'll just simply say they're us. In one way or another, the thoughts, mannerisms, behavior or lack thereof, and everything down to Elly and John Patterson's love handles is us. The only thing that *isn't* us is the actual day-to-day goings-on in the fictional family household. That stuff I make up. Also, my hair isn't like Elly's. Why hair is so important, I don't know, but as long as hers is long and mine is short, I can distance myself from her enough to say, "Absolutely that woman is *not* me." Then I have her do, say, think, and look the way I probably do, say, think, and look. Go figure.

People who've known Rod and me all our lives think they're keeping up with our actual family affairs by reading the strip, and who could blame them.

As I write, Rod is out in the back yard running his trains. It's 5 P.M. and he's been there since morning. He's wearing the same work shirt and pants he's worn in the shop for two weeks and

believes that as long as he changes his underwear daily, he's "decent." I've grown to love the way he looks on weekends.

Every so often, he comes into the house and asks if I'd like to "do something." It's important to do this because I've been known to harbor some resentment towards his hobby, and now and then on a Sunday I'd really *like* to do something. This is the predict-and-diffuse style of conflict avoidance, and Rod is an artist.

Another thing Rod knows about me is, I save up my nagging. Instead of nagging on a reasonable and regular basis, I allow multiple opportunities to build up to an incendiary degree. The slightest thing—a look, a remark, a foot on my couch space—can trigger an explosion of serious proportions, for which I will later apologize. He's learned not to take this stuff seriously. Thank heaven. Likewise, I sort of know when he needs to talk or to hit the sack early or just to be left alone. After a while, you read each other, you enjoy each other's talents, you allow each other's faults, and you recognize your own (hopefully)!

That's the kind of partnership Elly and John Patterson have. It's a good one.

If there's a thread that ties all of the stories and all of the characters in *For Better or For Worse*, together it's the relationship between Elly and John. Kids fight and bills pile up, work exhausts and time flies even when you aren't having any fun. Tempers and tantrums, egos and wants, and all the stuff that makes cohabitation with others so difficult becomes manageable when there is a stable and loving marriage at the center of it all. If there was a summary to this, if there's a statement to be made in what I do, it would be: Cherish your working partnerships. Take time to see all the good there is in the people you know and to expect the best in those you don't. Talk to your children and respect the intelligence in even the youngest child. Keep giving, even when you think you're not

getting back. Vote! Believe that there is a moral and a message in everything that happens to us, and that one individual can make a difference. Think of each person as a novel waiting to be read. I'm fifty-two and I'm only just learning all this stuff. I wonder why it's taken so long!

I wanted to say more about the people and places that appear in my work because I have been asked so many questions about them. The writing and the research have been a good thing. Now I know some of the answers!

I hope this book has helped to widen the door into the other world in which my families and I live. Please, don't knock. Just come in.

MMMMM

FOR ME, JOHN ... THIS TIME OF YEAR IS PURE HEAVEN!

THE SMELL, THE COLORS, THE MARKETS, THE COOL, FRESH WINDS.

OF ALL THE SEASONS—I THINK I LIKE THIS THE BEST.

WE'VE SEEN A LOT OF AUTUMNS TOGETHER, HAVEN'T WE, EL.

MORE THAN 20!

I GUESS YOU COULD SAY WE'RE IN THE "AUTUMN OF OUR LIVES!"

THAT'S A NICE ANALOGY, JOHN – COMPARING A LONG-LASTING RELATIONSHIP TO THIS TIME OF YEAR.

YEAH...

FOR ONE THING, THERE'S FEWER BUGS.